QUEST:

In Search of the Dragontooth

The Facsimile and Translation of the Journals of Magnalucius,
A Parable Wherein Things Are Revealed as Symbols
and Symbols are Found to be Real

Michael Green

Running Press
Philadelphia ◆ London

To Sally-of-the-soft-heart, who watched over
Magnalucius and provided him with kinder words
and sweeter company.

Readers who have enjoyed *Quest* may
also enjoy its prelude, *Unicornis*, an
investigation into the mysterious nature
of unicorns by Magnalucius, and tran-
scribed by Michael Green. *Unicornis* is
available from Running Press.

Canadian representatives: General Publishing Co., Ltd., 30 Lesmill Road, Don Mills, Ontario M3B 2T6.

9 8 7 6 5 4 3 2 1
Digit on the right indicates the number of this printing.

Library of Congress Cataloging-in-Publication Number 93–87405

ISBN 1–56138–413–5 (package)

Author's disclaimer: We make no claim for the veracity of the following account, and suggest that the
reader approach it as a work of allegorical fiction.

Cover design by E. June Roberts
Cover illustration by Michael Green
Interior design by Lili Schwartz
Latin translations by Jim O'Donnell
Edited by Melissa Stein
Typography: Galliard with AT Oxford by Deborah Lugar
Printed in China

This book may be ordered by mail from the publisher.
Please add $2.50 for postage and handling.
But try your bookstore first!

Running Press Book Publishers
125 South Twenty-second Street
Philadelphia, Pennsylvania 19103–4399

Contents

Introduction

 In the autumn of 1982, a cracked and brittle leather portfolio was presented to Running Press, a Philadelphia publisher. Inside was a wealth of yellowed, note-filled pages, delicately-tinted drawings, and several painted miniatures, all executed in a curious mixture of Medieval and Renaissance styles. Their tattered and discolored condition gave the appearance of great age and frequent reference. A rich legend accompanied them:

• They were the journals of a wandering sixteenth century artist-mystic named Magnalucius.

• As the Codex Unicornis, they were an heirloom of the Collegium Gnosticum, a secret gnostic brotherhood tracing its roots back to the ancient Desert Fathers.

• The Collegium was breaking centuries of silence and publishing these teachings because of a prophesy in the collection titled *The Last Days*:

The Last Days

THE UNICORN IS A *kindred race, bound to us in love and service. He points the way, he guard the gate, he waits until the End.*

Behold! An age shall come when science shall darken everywhere the hopes of men. Chariots of iron shall roll the land, which shall grow hard and barren to bear their weight. The air shall be filled with a clamor of many voices. Unknown plagues and sicknesses shall arise. The sphere of the Moon shall bear the booted heels of Man.

Mighty kingdoms will contend for all the world, and turn against it, until the soil and the sea shall sicken and the wind become a flux of poisoned vapors. And all men shall be sorely tried, so that at the last, none may escape the choice between Light and Darkness.

Then, in the Time of Great Purification, will the Unicorn return, lingering at the margins of our realm, to seed our minds with dreams of a brighter age to come; and many shall hunger to see him. But being a spiritual creature, the Unicorn must conform himself to the images held

in the hearts of those who call him forth. And there shall be so many ill-formed and conflicting ideas as to his nature, that he can hardly find a way to satisfy them all.

Then must these pages be revealed and broadcast without restraint; that all confusion may be resolved and a single vision call forth the Unicorn in his true, original, and perfect state.

Running Press recognized the manuscript's worth and was keen to publish a facsimile edition. English-Latin translations were carefully edited to maintain the flavor of the original work.

The Magnalucius notebooks of Part I were first published in North America under the title *Unicornis* and were enthusiastically received.

The Unicorn has a singular virtue: he can penetrate
our dreams and there address us. Therefore take
heed, O Dreamer, when the Unicorn appears to
thee. Though his speech is unlike any tongue of
Man, yet shalt thou comprehend!

However, the story was not over. Ten years after the Unicornis Manuscript first came to light, Pavilion Publishers in Great Britain was approached by an aristocratic young man offering to sell a bundle of antique illustrated journals which he had discovered behind a medieval Italian altarpiece, along with a curious glass amulet. He had, he claimed, offered the artifacts to the Bodleian at Oxford University, but had been rebuffed for lack of any authenticating documents. He resolved to publish the collection, and so let the public be the judge. It was indeed handsome enough for publication, and a deal was struck.

A widely read junior editor soon discerned that the work had been executed by the same hand that had crafted *Unicornis*, and apparently formed a sequel to that work.

As the pages were translated and put in order, it became plain that they described a search for the whereabouts of a "*Perilous Dragontooth.*" Furthermore, if the document could be believed, this Dragontooth might *still be buried somewhere in Britain*. No acumen was needed to see that publishing these journals would encourage many readers to seek and claim it, much in the manner of various popular treasure-hunting books which capture the public's imagination from time to time. In fact, the journals themselves end with an invitation—a plea—to some reader in the future to find the Tooth. Was this a centuries-old quest which, unfinished, extended right into the present time?

Debate was vigorous among those who were shown the manuscript: was this a forgery? An allegory? A few were convinced that an actual relic lay somewhere in England waiting to be found. Others were certain the whole thing was a fraud. It became a passion among them to settle the dispute, and they began gathering regularly after hours to puzzle over the document. The task was not easy. Many folios were damaged or missing altogether. Furthermore, the author had often taken pains to conceal his own deductions. But this only increased the puzzle's fascination, and hastened the next turn of fate.

After many weeks, the possible whereabouts of the Tooth were determined, and the team set out to find it. At the site, a metal detector quickly indicated *something* beneath the ground, so they dug, and

 unearthed a casket. Kneeling on the ground, they carefully pried it open, and were astonished to find inside *a huge blackened tusk mounted in a corroded bronze handle.* Here was the Perilous Dragontooth! Reaching down to remove the tusk, they found that it was wedged firmly into its container—none could dislodge it.

Reviewing the manuscript, it was obvious that *they* were not the "Rightful Finder"—only that person could remove the Tooth. No, the One Rightful Finder had yet to be discovered.

Read on then, and *let the Quest begin!*

PART I.

The Discovery of the Unicorn

BEING A FACSIMILE AND translation of the Lost Journals of Magister Magnalucius, portions having been first presented as *UNICORNIS*, but here arranged in a more accurate manner.

Planting begun in earnest, but I must record a singular event. Shortly after daybreak, as is my habit, I walked in contemplation through the alder groves bordering our river. There I glimpsed a forest creature altogether white in color—a hart, I now believe, but cannot be certain, for it was moving through thickest brush all greening with new leaves. Now this was the remarkable thing: I was balanced in a most inward state of devotion, yet this curious creature did not draw my attention outward, as is the irksome habit of intriguing objects. Instead, I stood awhile in a most pleasurable still-ness of mind and spirit; for the beast seemed as much within me as without, among the alders. But when my curiosity quickened enough to speculate on what species of creature I beheld, it vanished forthwith.

FROM *The Unicornis Notebooks of Magnalucius*

May the loving God protect us and our Master.

The First Sunday after Easter

About the second hour of the morning, Sylvanius, our excellent cook, was seated at the edge of the forest that overlooks our garden. Not far away, I was gathering herbs and greenery for the cure of fever. Now Sylvanius was deep in contemplation, as is his custom, when there approached him a white creature. There could be no mistake— its single horn was white and shining: it was a unicorn. In full view it stood, only a few paces from Sylvanius, regarding him as silently as the fall of dew.

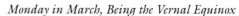

Whether the cook saw the animal or not, I could not tell, for Sylvanius made no outward sign or motion. For near an hour the two remained thus, Man and Unicorn, neither moving at all. Nor did I budge from where I watched, awestruck.

There was a slight odor of spice, like cinnamon. I do now believe that Sylvanius and the creature were conversing, one with the other, in the brightness of their minds.

hordeum 3 modii — ⸻ grossi 7· soldini 3
triticum rusum/ 4 modii ⸻ grossi 12
hordeum coctum, 1 dolium ⸻ grossi 4
rapum plaustrum plenum ⸻ grossi 3 soldini 1

Omnia Eum Laudans

Feria secunda (a.d. Kal. apr.)

Aequinoctia Vernalis

Seminationes inceptae revera. Aliquod curiosum: Bene mane,
ut mihi solet, in contemplatione dulci per dumeta alboga
citra flumen ambulabam — ibi conspexi bestiam silvarum
miram, albam omnino. Cervus quidam erat, ut nunc
credo sed non certum dicere possum quia erat ille videndus
per frondes densissimas. Sed hoc miraculum grandior.

Plenus eram intimo orationis spiritu quando illud vidi
sed hic visus non me extrahebat ab orationibus ab
orationibus meis ut solet per curiositatem ad res
novas visas.

Per contra, hic visus valde me leniebat et ekvebat
ad quoddam libramen animae cum mente. Huic
ibi diu steteram magna cum securitate.
Visus videbatur esse iam intra me quam extra.

Sed cum deinde inquirerem et specularem de quo genere
bestia ille veniret, statim evanuit.

Deus omnes nos protegat et magistram nostram

I do not dare speak to anyone of this mystery. Rather, I shall await the return of our Master, who can untangle this for me, for he is a man learned in all the knowledge that men possess, and more besides.

Friday, March the 26th

Again I have glimpsed the white beast, and I marvel at God's works, for I strongly suspect it is the fabled Unicorn!

Having finished tilling the westernmost field and leaning on my spade, I fell to gazing on a great vine of honeysuckle in new bloom upon the ruined wall. Upon me, unbidden, came a speechless joy at that Divine Hand that guides to perfection every stem and leaf and petal; and I was lifted up and saw the flowery mass as never before, glowing with a celestial and jewel-like light.

How long I gazed thus, I know not, but at length I grew mindful that in the center of this extraordinary sight was the head of an animal, regarding me with great kindly eyes that showed no fear. On his forehead was set a single horn, white as ice. The sight of this singular device sent a thrill up my back. I believe I swooned, for the next I knew I was sitting on the earth, and the creature was no more to be seen.

I know it will not be wise to speak of this hastily.

The Wednesday Following

The mystery of this beast has seized my heart! All my wanderings and secret studies have not stirred me so deeply. I feel as if I stood on the deck of a noble ship and gazed upon a foreign land in which are seen strange adventures and wondrous deeds.

Yet this is no ordinary obsession, for my thoughts bring me a rare tranquillity, almost a joy. I seem to catch sight of this truth: the Unicorn is not the true center of this mystery. For although this creature is most manifestly sensible and corporeal, yet at the same time I know he is a kind of sign, a portent.

Such are my thoughts; for today, a little after first light, I saw the creature again, and I shall tell how. Wandering father afoot than usual, I came to the twin hills overlooking the vineyard. In that abundant meadow, I was so taken by the quiet and beauty of the Lord's creation (all in the flush of springtime), that I threw myself down upon the grass and then, lying back like a child, looked up at the sky. Gazing at the clouds that sailed overhead, I fell into a reverie.

Some time after, I sensed a fragrance, as of cinnamon. And sitting upright, lo! I saw the favored beast, all shining and not many paces away. And for this first time I heard his voice, solemn yet musical, like a distant bell echoing in a tall tower.

Then turning himself, the unicorn walked into the small grove of trees that crowns the slope, and I could see him no longer. I followed after (for it seemed that I should), but nowhere in the copse did I find him. But neither could the animal have fled unseen, for those trees are everywhere surrounded by open meadow; nor is there any hiding place among them.

Of this matter I am amazed. Yet shall I continue my silence.

Sunday, April the 11th

As I labored in the fields this day I heard voices calling that our Master had at last finished his long retreat. I ran to greet him, hoping to beg for his private counsel on the matter of this perplexing beast that so dominates my thoughts.

Others were already with him, but as I hurried up, he turned to me, saying loudly that all might hear, "And hast thou seen the Unicorn?"

I had forgotten that from him, no secrets are concealed. So great was my consternation that all I could reply was simply, "Yes."

"At last!" he cried. "And dost thou think that thou alone hast seen the creature?"

Then all the others laughed, but not with ill intent, and left me standing in confusion.

Wednesday, April the 14th

Our Master came upon me by the ruined fountain and bade me speak.

"What is this Unicorn," I asked, "that he may disappear?"

"The beast cannot disappear," Eugnostos replied. "He merely leaves our realm and passes to another."

I asked, "What other realm is there?"

"Hast thou no knowledge of the Four Ages?" he inquired of me.

(Which knowledge I did have from the writings of Plato; the first being the fabled Golden Age, then the Ages of Silver and of Bronze, and now, lastly a final Age of Iron.)

And our Master asked me: "Are these Four Ages not akin to the great dynasties that chart the failing history of mankind?"

"They are," I replied.

"And yet they are not!" he said. "Or rather, more than that."

23

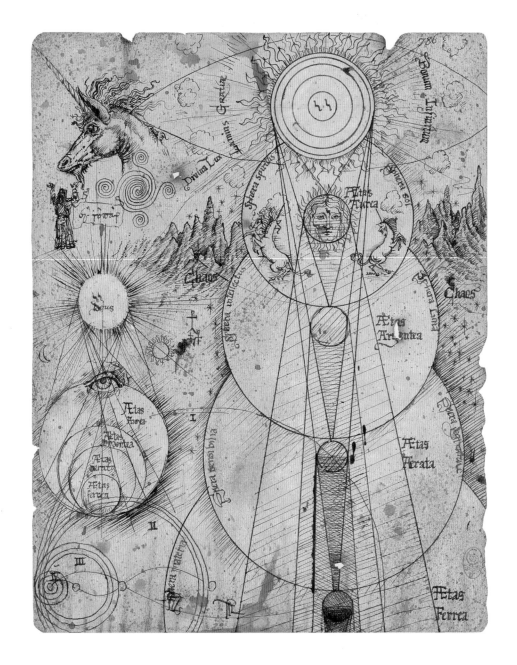

Then he led me into the garden and seated me on the Bench of Learning, and covered my head with is own cloth, and instructed me. I am confounded, for he gave me a great teaching in whose light all things are seen anew.

"Attend well," he said. "*Each of these previous ages continues still,* for they were not measures of the changing years upon this world we know, but rather are other realms where Man has sojourned before arriving here.

"The first is called the Age of Gold, because it is as radiant with golden light as a thought newborn from the mind of God. Each age that follows is a further elaboration of that theme; there being three more steps by which divine thought is finally congealed into our Age's dense and inert matter. Altogether, the realms are as the four notes of a powerful chord that spans all that was, or is, or ever shall be.

"Man has occupied each realm and, each time failing in his oath and promise, was removed to a lower, coarser one. The others are invisible to us—yet every age endures, intermingling with the rest, the warp of one serving as the other's woof."

As Eugnostos spoke, a great stillness had come over the garden. Standing quietly by the trees was the Unicorn, his eyes wide and bright, his ears attentive as my Master continued his account:

"Know thou," he said to me, "that the Unicorn is a creature of the Golden Age, which is his proper home. But as the enduring friend of Man, often he joins us in our exile, for he can cross the threshold of the ages. And when he departs from us, he does not disappear, but simply passes through a portal."

Then I asked: "May we pass through these portals also?"

"Indeed!" the blessed Eugnostos replied. "No man can regain the paradise from whence he came, except that he journey back across those realms. Yea, many have passed therein. Their gates are never far, though the realms are artfully concealed, the finer within the coarser, and each entrance is a riddle difficult to discover without the proper guide. For some, the Unicorn serves as guide. *And he has chosen thee!*"

Saturday, of May the Beginning

Last night I returned alone, weary of travel, and under the starlight gave most wholehearted thanks to God for this domain where we find such sweet refuge! My brief sojourn in Firenze left me in bafflement and disarray. But today I clearly see how that city's magnificent intellectual ferment is but the flush of a fever arising from a bottomless emptiness of faith.

Those noble men, many of them my friends and fellow students of old, all vie to surpass one another and profess mastery of things of which they dwell in utter ignorance. To think that the beauty of their frail works can conquer death! And at the core of all their ceaseless activities lies a discontent so profound that it grieves my heart.

To none of them did I speak of the precious Unicorn, for their proud minds would have considered him either a fanciful myth or a scientific curiosity. Even so, I caused them great amusement, for to their eyes I have become a child again, a superstitious rustic clinging to dim fables in this age of changing ways and bold discovery. If these men are to shape the years to come, then my heart cries out, for those times will prove harsh and inhospitable to our modest, friendly creature and his subtle ways—driving him to retreat still further from the paths of Man.

But let others mold the world! Tomorrow, at last, I go into my retreat.

Sunday, May the 2nd; at Dawn

Eugnostos has bidden that I take with me neither paper nor pen. I here confess that my past seclusions have been mostly dry and difficult, largely relieved by my books and writings. Yet I must now trust my Master.

Eugnostos says: "Only when thou drinkest from the rivers of silence wilt thou learn to sing."

Sunday, May the 9th

Have I not heard the tale of the man who dug for turnips and found gold? My retreat is done!

For years I have tempered my mind with the divine art of alchemy, bathed in the mystical teachings of the Emerald Tablet, probed the secrets of Kabbalistic doctrine, sojourned with the anchorites of Scete. But now I have met the Unicorn face to face, and I am undone; for nothing had prepared me for the fiery touch of his wondrous mind.

Three days I passed in reverie and prayer, until at last I sat in sunlight by my open door, and I was content; and he came at last and laid his thoughts on mine. And I, willing and trusting, moved with them, filled with sweetness and strange images, seemingly from times so remote as to be beyond reckoning. Finally I could contain no more, and his touch began to burn too brightly. I was overcome, but the creature withdrew and vanished from my sight.

·SILVA·BROCILEANDENSIS·

Now I understand the secret of that little hut, and why all our company displays such eagerness to retire there. For the Unicorn must dwell nearby—or could it be that a portal to his secret realm is not far hence?

After that first meeting I saw the Unicorn each day—but no more will I write, but this: here is an ancient mystery beyond compare. And yet the creature (can this be true?) *is now my friend.*

Says Eugnostos: "In friendship, there is no other goal but the uncovering of the spirit."

Tuesday, May the 11th

 After the noon meal, the blessed Eugnostos called me to his chamber. He asked me why I supposed there exist no true accounts of the Unicorn and answered himself, saying, "The Unicorn is not drawn to clerics and philosophers like ourselves, but rather to the youthful and innocent. Those few scholars fated to meet the magical beast were marvelously emptied of their burdensome learning and were ever after disinclined to write or speak of their encounters—for the memory of the Unicorn is like a shining taper that words would only dim."

Then Eugnostos smiled as if amused, saying, "But I see some special destiny has singled out thee to do this work."

"What work?" I asked, not comprehending.

"Doth not thy hand still crave to write and draw? Then write and draw thou must, and record the truth and history of the Unicorn. It seems that a divine purpose is here to be revealed, and thy skill may bear great fruit in the end. Work diligently, and let us look to a swift conclusion of the whole labor. But be not indiscreet, and keep the work secret. Hast thou not seen the sad fate of thy several friends, so dazzled by their own gifts that, unknowing, they have lost their way?"

Then our Master discharged me of all my other duties and bade me go and write. Thus humbled, but exhilarated, I departed his chamber.

In Thee Is Concealed a Strange and Terrible Mystery.

Ego Magnalucius, Anchianae vilnae natus a.n.s. MCDLVII . . . I Magnalucius, born in 1457, set forth this work in my own hand and attest to its veracity. By God's grace, I have not lacked education, having first learned the art of drawing. But in its inks and pigments I found only pride and emptiness. So I turned to books of natural philosophy and alchemy, even to the sacred Kabbala of the Hebrews. The most profound teachings of the Gnostic brethren I pursued in the cities and monasteries of Egypt. And in all these studies I learned hidden secrets, many and great.

Yet all I learned in those years was as a shadow in the light of the Unicorn, whose coming set the keystone to all my knowledge. All before had been first fruits, now harvest abounding.

Now this work pays no heed to the vain fancies and foolish imaginings of anyone, though they may have acquired the weight of hallowed tradition. As says Saint Columban, flower of the cloisters of Ireland: "Manifestly ancient is error, but the truly ancient is truth." If common lore long asserted by the wise and accepted by the majority is here contradicted, let the reader be satisfied that these words and pictures are witness to pure and simple experience, and judge the truth for himself.

O Reader: If thou art neither scribe nor sacrificer, cast not thy gaze upon this book, for it contains secret teachings useful only to the few and troubling to the many. And if thou seekest only mere amusement, read no further. But if thou art an earnest pilgrim on the path of Life, then open, read, and ponder.

Mind on Mind In Wordless Thought, These Things The Unicorn Made Known to Me:

The Book of Generation

The creature's true origins lie in the depths of Time, in that beginningless Beginning when all was emptiness and waste, darkness and mist. Then moved the Holy One to sunder the dark from the bright. So were established concord and balance, with darkness driven to the fringes and the Abode of Light at the middle point of all.

De Historia et Veritate Unicornis

Mysterium Tremendum in te occultatum

Ego Magnalucius, Anchsanne villae natus
A.D. MCDLVII, hoc opus mea manu
scripturam affero at Veritatem eius attestor:
Institutione non minimus (Deo Gratias) artem
quae graphice vocatur adeptus eram sed in pig-
mentis et atramentis & eius artis repperi saltim
modo superbiam, et inanitatem. Et ideo tunc deui
ad libros philosophorum: philosophiae naturalis operam
dei, et alchimiae, et quidem habui sancta a Iudae-
orum, necnon et doctrinis futurorum magicorum
profundissimas, dum peregrentis in civitate & apud
Egyptiacos. Ab qua terra iamdudum habitavi. In
omnibus quibus didici occulta et arcana multa et
magna.

Multa igitur per illos annos didici mihi adherant tant-
am luminis quantum postea imperi per subigeram
mihi invidias. Tenebrae illuminant & fortulsit. Per
eius adiutorium experi aliquid tantum omni doctrina mea
affini, quae huc tenus primi die fuerant in hunc magis abundans.

Hoc opus respicit ad nullas fantasias et imagines
ludicras aliquorum hominum, quamvis grandes relata
et antiquioribus asseveratae te sint. Error non in
veritas si tantum antiquas, ut ait sanctus Columbanus
flos claustrorum Hiberniae. Manifeste antiquum est
error, sed semper sit iunior aet veritas.

Si nunc contradicenda sunt, multa ne dicit te sapien-
tium tam diu damnare. Benevolus lector animae sciat
quia veritas ex tabulae huius operis attestantur
experientiae meae tam recenti quam frequenti
quisque veritatem sibi iudicat.

Nisi antiquarius vel quasi mathetes sis
in hunc librum ne oculos ponas.
Habet doctrinam arcanum, paucis quidem
utilem, multis vero perturbantem.

Qui vultis artium gaudium inane
desinas ineptire. Ne porro legas.

Qui per viam vitae peregrinaris tolle lege pondera.

But darkness, once given a situation and compass for itself, grew weighty beyond accounting, intruding among all things and drawing them toward itself according to their weights and inclinations.

Therefore was the balance made to tremble, and from that trembling arose a resonance—an awesome sound that circled in the vast emptiness, chanting mightily. The holy One modulated that sound to make of it a chord of great sweetness, and breathed into it intelligence, so that it might become a spirit of harmony and guidance unto every corner of the void. This was the powerful spirit called Galgallim, whirling itself through uncounted ages while ever spiraling around the central Light. And while some things still fell into darkness, yet Galgallim guided others on a more rarified path toward the shores of Light. In such a way was balance achieved once more.

Then the Holy One wished for a panel on which to display His greater art; and between the shores of Light and the walls of darkness He hung in balance the Earth. Its naked mountains he raised in fire and scattered them with shining gems that still reflect those flames. Then the Holy One addressed the spirit of guidance, which is Galgallim, saying, "Out of the hidden gulfs I made thee, free and by form unbounded. Wilt thou accept shape upon Earth, that thou mayst supply a service even greater?"

And even as it was asked, so it was agreed.

The First Unicorn

WRAPPED IN A CLOUD came he, by a bright whirlwind borne along. He descended gently from the heavens to the infant fields of Earth, even before the fires of its forming were yet subdued. Thus did the Unicorn possess the brightness of the Light, that he might drive all darkness and obscurity from him. He was called Asallam, of unicorns the firstborn, a creature fearfully wrought and wonderful to behold, bearing a horn of spiral light that is the sign of Galgallim, the guide.

Final Entry

WHAT GOOD FORTUNE! I have just been requested, by the most formal letter, to address a group of "my most esteemed colleagues" in Firenze on the subject of my recent "exploits." Are these the same people who for years have been so condescending toward my pursuits? How time and Fate doth change all things. Already I can think of nothing other than my presentation. It must be rich, but subtle, for these luminaries will not be able to digest the full import of my Hermetic discoveries at first taste. Only the most attuned will be aware that I shall be establishing the foundation for a new philosophy, a *lapis philosophorum novum*. Perhaps a small study group may evolve—but one that no doubt will have great influence!

Curiously, Eugnostos was not particularly inspired by the prospect; perhaps he did not grasp the full significance. But I pressed him for his blessing (am I a child that I need his permission for every jaunt?) and finally, he gave it, in his sober way: "Do what you wish," he said. "May God be with you. Too much sugar turns some tongues toward salt. But we will meet again." Must he always speak in riddles? It is not as if I shall be gone more than a fortnight. I must go and pack.

(Here end the selections from *The Unicornis Notebooks of Magnalucius.*)

PART II.
In Search of the Dragontooth

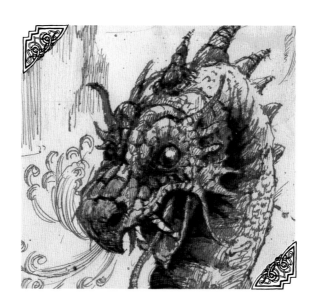

O YOU WHO IN a future time discover these journals and peruse within: may your heart be lifted and informed by the Quest which here lies before you, but let not its wonders inflame you beyond true wisdom. For as I have learned from great toil, *things are not always what they seem.*—Magnalucius.

January the 21st

I have been commanded to write again, so write I will.

What urge brought me back to this place of dreams? I had not expected Eugnostos to be alive. Yet beyond hope he was. The rains arrived along with me, beating on the thick panes of the old palazzo, and I sat by a fire in the main hall for a day, waiting for a summons to see the master, while every now and then someone would whisper in the colonnade, *Did you see him? He has come back.*

What carried me away? Restlessness? Foolishness? Fate? How fearlessly a man will plunge into snare and delusion! When did this place seem something that I must grow beyond? When did I cease yearning for the ancient taste of grace? When did the Unicorn cease his visits? Surely, I thought, my heart should tremble in anticipation of seeing the old master again. But it did not—a token, perhaps, of the passing years.

The Book of Redtooth, or The Quest Notebooks of Magnalucius

Yet when I finally walked down the red flagstones to his study, I confess my heart quickened, and when I opened that familiar polished door it was with a nervous hand.

He sat in his accustomed seat by the leaded windows. "My son," he said, as if no time at all had passed since we last met, "how are you? What news do you bring? Did you see the old cypress fell across the chamomile beds? It must be removed at once."

He had aged. His skin seemed almost transparent now, but his eyes still shone like those of a curious child. Suddenly (as of old) his demeanor changed and he became the Ancient One. "So," he said in a soft voice, "you have wandered the world and tasted the ten thousand things. But did your feet ever really touch the ground? Magnalucius, it is time now to start the work in earnest."

And so it began anew.

I sought instruction. "Do what you wish," said Eugnostos. I sat to pray in the tiny oratory—till I saw that I was mostly gazing out the window. So I chopped up the cypress. I scoured pots, I repaired the fresco in the hall. Now for a week I have done little but stroll the empty gardens along the river and beat the borders of the estate. Yet a great *shift* is taking place within me.

This morning Eugnostos called me to his study. He was taking ewe's milk cheese and pungent olives from a small tray, and invited me to partake as well. We ate in silence punctuated by regular clinks as he spat his pits into a brass urn. Eugnostos, ever the peasant!

"You know," he said, wiping his mouth, "someone who has not found the well cannot draw the water, eh Magnalucius? And someone who has not found the earth cannot dig a well."

"Sir?"

"I have just learned (he gestured to an opened letter upon his desk) the whereabouts of a certain relic for which I have long searched. It is a talisman of greatest worth, a treasure in fact, lost for centuries. But it has shown itself at last and is now in safe-keeping at ———."

"The monastery?"

"—which lies some distance from here as you know. I have need for an emissary who can conduct himself there without incident and procure the thing."

I nodded.

"It must then be delivered safely to Nural Din the Andalusian. Have you heard of this physician? Such a splendid scholar! Such a loss for Spain."

"I recall the name."

"Good. I have thought it over and it seems best to employ an old traveler like you. What do you say? Will you be my ambassador?"

"But my lord!" I cried, "In returning here I have ceased my wanderings."

"Magnalucius, I do not propose a wandering. This is your master's work. And perhaps you will find some benefit in the undertaking as well."

terra profectus est. Cutis eius erat paene perlucida
sicut vitrum, sed oculi eius vim mutabant sicut pulcherum
curioforum. Statim, sicut longe antea, mutatusque est
in factus est sicut antiquus ille.

cum murmur a die
ergo mundum

Ω

Peregrinati
et decem
mille formas
vitae cognati.
Redesne aliqua
Dextri stabili
gradu aliquando
erant?
Maena lucius.
Iam tandem
incipiendam
est kum arbitror
tibi opus

Et sicut
factum
est de nouo.

≈≈≈

My heart protested and I thought to refuse him, but instead I asked, "What is this treasure?"

"Do you remember once in your meditations you came upon a *fall* of *periadams*?"

"I remember. They gleamed like jewels, but did not last the day."

"So it is with the *dew* of the Unicorn," said he. "But three great periadams in antiquity had the virtue of endurance, and our treasure is one of them. It is the lost Periadam, called Hesed the Abiding."

"Then I will go," said I.

"When you arrive at the monastery," said Eugnostos, "find *Brother Severinus.* Give him my name and he will deliver to you the Hesed." He handed me a small ebony box. "Seal it in here, and deliver it to Nural Din with these words: *Find the Thinker not the thought. Behold the treasure men have sought.*"

"And where?"

"By marvelous coincidence, my beloved," said he, "Nural Din is now house physician at the very estate where your illustrious brother—or is it half-brother?—has just found patronage."

I was dumbstruck. "What? Are they familiars?"

Eugnostos made a dismissive gesture with his hand. "Not at all. Have you not grown accustomed to such correspondences on our path? Do you not see that you have been caught up in a grand pattern?

"But how do you have such intimate knowledge of my kinsfolk?"

"*The affairs of my children are my affairs,* Magnalucius. Now go, find and deliver the Periadam. You will visit your brother of course. But remember: *All knowledge is vain, except where there be work. And all work is empty, except where there be love.* And one more thing, my son. Start a journal again for this adventure."

How did the old man know I had ceased keeping accounts? That is the mystery of Eugnostos, and the reason why I do his bidding again, after all these years.

 Leaving comfort and repose, I depart in the morning with ninety-nine gold florins from Eugnostos—an extravagant sum for such a trip. I shall need but little of it.

February the 5th

I first spied the monastery of ———— from afar, at midday, ancient and sprawling among the hills, but it was vespers before I arrived at its mossy gates. Alas! I learned from the door-warden that Friday last, Severinus, his assistant, and the Abbot all perished in a mountain landslide returning from Lemieux. May they rest in peace! I will be presented to the new abbot in the morning. I was served a simple meal of tart cheese, barley bread, and gravy in their cavernous kitchen and conducted across the cloister to a room in the cellarium. The bells are ringing for compline, and I must snuff my taper.

February the 6th

Today, at midmorning, a young monk ushered me down a long cloister to a courtyard filled with herbs and flowers leafing early in the warmth of the sheltering stone. Abbot Longinus sat on a bench by the far wall, his head tilted back to the sun. I took a seat on a bench nearby. His monk bowed and left.

"You are the visitor called Magnalucius conveying the greetings of an Eugnostos of Bologna?" He spoke in the vernacular Italian of the region.

"Of Brescia."

He gave a wave of his hand. "No matter. I do not know him." The man's face was pleasant, but he had the watery eyes found in elderly monks who have not been bothered by an original thought in decades.

He squinted at me. "Did he send a letter of passage?"

"No," I replied. "He said that the mention of his name to Brother Severinus would suffice as introduction."

He gave a long sigh. "You know of the most unfortunate accident?"

"I was informed last night."

43

"It was a terrible thing. How inexplicable are the ways of the Lord." He stroked his beard. "I am sorry, for I see you have traveled far. Please feel you can rest here before continuing your way." He shut his eyes and leaned back into the sun, signaling that the interview was over.

I had no choice but to pursue the matter: "Perhaps, Reverend Abbot, my purpose might still be fulfilled. You see, Brother Severinus had something in his keeping. . . ."

"*Something in his keeping?*" He spoke with an exaggerated weariness. "Impossible. His was a life of poverty; he left neither will nor effects. I cannot help you."

He was hiding the truth, I was sure of it, and I resolved to try a ploy.

"Of course," said I. "I am at fault. I should have brought the proper documentation. The Curia will understand."

Longinus suddenly awoke. "The Curia?"

"I have been charged with a most vital—and secret—research into something of great interest here."

"There are many things to study in this world, my friend, but most of them are of little interest to good Christian men."

"Of course," said I. "But the holy fathers have a burden greater than that of their flock. Did not the Lord imbue all things in His creation with a lesson to be studied? The pig's gluttony or the purity of the swan are qualities for any man to observe. But it is the sacred duty of my superiors to overlook nothing on earth, to consider what hidden meaning even the more . . . *novel* . . . thing would reveal, seen through the eye of wisdom. Of course, without the guidance of the Holy Church the strange and mysterious are mere curiosities. Or worse. Believe me when I say innocent-seeming things can lead the unwary straight to the Deceiver. But I am sure your Holiness already knows all this, and your discretion is well-advised."

He cleared his throat. "Please. I cannot accept such honorifics. But I see you are not a common seeker of grotesqueries. Yes, there is such a study as you delineate, though a dangerous one."

"But those are the very words of Cardinal Mandrona!" said I.

The old man frowned and blinked and stroked his chin. "Then I will reveal to you this has not always been well understood by my esteemed predecessors. Excessive holiness can cloud a man's judgment. Discretion is essential. The contents of the Antiquarium must be kept secret."

Antiquarium? I suppressed my excitement. "Of course," I responded. "And well I understand that it is a . . . shall I say. . . ."

"A source of embarrassment for our establishment? You may speak freely. Yes, it is true. For centuries it has drawn a rogue's parade of pilgrims. Yet Severinus (may he rest in peace) did not realize this danger."

"It is well," said I, "that the Antiquarium remain the domain of those who, like yourself, are not so easily deluded."

"One must be careful these days," he said solemnly. He motioned that I was to assist him to his feet. "Come, let us look about."

He led me through the colonnade, down some stairs, and through an ill-lit passageway, and unlocked the door of a dusty storeroom. At the far end he fit another key into a closet door, which, to my surprise, opened into a narrow stair. He reached behind the door and found a gold chain hung with an intricately worked broach of Celtic design.

"The builder and first warden of the Antiquarium was Glinne the Learned. Every succeeding warden was carefully chosen from among our monks, and was schooled in its contents and lore. It was a position of great honor, but secret, for the same reasons then as now. Alas, the lineage is broken, for Severinus was the warden, and his apprentice fell with him, as did Abbot Ignacius. As senior of the brothers, I act as abbot now, and until I find the right man, I must guard the Antiquarium as well."

So saying, Longinus put the chain over his neck with little ceremony, and proceeded up the stairs. Reaching the top, he uttered the most pitiable cry.

I bounded to his aid. "Good sir," I cried, "what ails you?"

"The room! See! And I the abbot now!"

 We stood on the threshold of a small, musty, eight-sided room in total disarray. It was lined with cabinets, but their doors were all forced open, their contents strewn about the floor. The place had been invaded. "A thief?" I asked.

45

"No, no," he replied, waving his hands, "there is no way. I have the only key."

"Did not Brother Severinus have a key?" I asked.

"Of course," he replied, "but by rule it never left his side, and therefore perished with him beneath the landslide. What am I to do? Surely this is the work of evil spirits!"

Spirits or burglars, the poor man was quite undone.

"Good sir," I said, steadying him, "I have been trained extensively as a librarian and I have long studied the Natural Sciences under the highest ecclesiastical authorities. Accept my services in restoring order here. Perhaps God has set me before you for a purpose other than I thought."

The man immediately brightened. "Yes, mysterious are His ways. The Antiquarium must be put right. But tell none of the brethren. It is unnecessary to disturb them."

I continued, "And if we apply holy waters about this place in accordance with the canons of St. Celibius, we shall never fear demonic intrusions again."

"Yes, yes," said he, his simple face brightening, "Blessed St. Celibius."

With little more words than these, the Abbot gratefully laid the Antiquarium and its exorcism in my hands, and left. Thus, aided by the good Celibius (whom I must confess was invented for the occasion), I found myself alone in the ravaged room. Had this ransacking been a search for the Periadam? Could it still be here? The sheer disarray gave me encouragement; the hunt had been conducted with considerably less care than mine would be. Scattered all about was a fabulous debris: here were fragments of a weathered stone dragon; an ivory basilisk; a great egg set on a silver tripod; dried skins of unknown origin; even a scaled and taloned foot inside a crystal casket. A tiny Persian painting showed a great serpent wrapped about an azure mountain; a tapestry hung on the far wall depicted a dragon and unicorn in mortal combat. In all, for me it was an earthly paradise, but for my fears that the Periadam was stolen, and a suspicion that Severinus's death was no accident.

February the 10th

 This morning I told Longinus that I wished to draw up clearly definable classes and categories among the objects, and he happily sent me to the monastery parchmenter to procure a binding for the catalog. While examining his paper, the fellow, thinking I knew more of the Antiquarium than I did, made a caustic remark about Severinus's trade with the papal library: an early copy of Aristotle's *Poetics* had been exchanged for some trifling curio for the museum. The man was angling me for details. Feigning ignorance, I made my escape.

Discovered an extraordinary bestial footprint impressed in stone, the teeth of a Manticore, the dried penis of a sea serpent, a jewel from the forehead of a Naga of the Indies (this last obviously a fabrication). One's mind spins before this assembly of wonders . . . but no sign of the Periadam.

February the 11th

This afternoon Longinus came to check on my progress. When I remarked on the great age of some of the artifacts, he responded with some pride that the Antiquarium had been started the year of their blessed founder's death, that being all of nine hundred and two years ago. I wondered if the collection included a periadam, but he had never heard of such a thing. Later he returned with some papers he had discovered in the old abbot's apartments. They seem to be a manifest of all acquisitions to this collection over the past seventeen years. The Periadam is not listed.

My hope is this: If Severinus intended to pass the Periadam along to Eugnostos, then might he have hidden it secretly, rather than displaying it with the regular collection?

February the 13th

Before, shadows. Now the sun. Here is the tale: I had lit a lamp to examine the last relic for the day, a small limestone pillar carved as intertwined serpents. I saw that its capital was a separate piece socketed into the column. Bracing the shaft between my knees, I turned the top. There was a hollow scraping sound, the smell of stone dust, and off it came! The shaft was hollow, and I withdrew from it a velvet-wrapped package. Ah! Inside, I found what I sought, the Periadam, shining and pure!

But would Longinus release the thing? Never. I slipped the stone under my cap and crept away. I had not come for my own purposes. Let the blame of theft fall upon my master. He will disperse it by his own lights. In that moment I became an acolyte of Hermes, Master of Trickery. *Messenger of the gods!*

Spent the morning pondering a delicate problem while putting the Antiquarium into order: having led Longinus to permit this study, how could I leave abruptly, the task half done, without arousing his suspicions? Longinus himself came to my rescue after offices. He asked if I would consider taking vows and becoming warden of the Anti- quarium. I responded with the greatest enthusiasm, but affirmed that I must first ask Rome. He seemed greatly pleased, and said I should make preparations for leaving immediately. Of course I agreed, telling him I would send word from Rome. Onward!

March the 10th

It was a pleasant enough journey to the palatial estate where this Nural Din is employed. Winter was banished as I descended into this sweetest of fertile plains. Spring had aroused the land. Peasants sang in the fields and everywhere green vines twined up their arbors.

Nural Din has done well for himself. Upon arrival at his master's palazzio, I was escorted down tapestried halls to a study that rivaled any I have seen in Firenze. Everywhere was the soft gleam of polished wood and brocaded fabrics—indeed, there was a certain excess of luxury which I found questionable in the quarters of one whom I had supposed to be exalted in the Brotherhood.

But the books! There before me two long walls were lined with all the writings of the seven ages. In this princely hoard was *Libro de Magika Sacrada* of Abra-Melin the Mage, *De Clavicules Salomonis* by Anselm of Morimondo, the *Legemeton* of Silius the

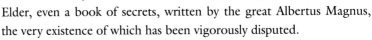 Elder, even a book of secrets, written by the great Albertus Magnus, the very existence of which has been vigorously disputed.

Thus engrossed I was startled by a discreet feminine cough on the other side of the room. I turned and saw, peeking from behind a stack of books on a writing table, the tip of a pale gray cap and a pearled hairnet. I was not aware that any of our order was wedded. Had I come upon my host's mistress? The thought alarmed me, and I fear I simply stood there dumbly until the woman rose from behind the desk. She was tall, with raven hair, and was dressed in a dark velvet court gown. She moved to meet me with an air of elegance, holding her hand out to mine. "Greetings, Magnalucius," she said in flawless Latin, "I see you are an admirer of books." I nodded. "Then while you are here, feel free to pursue your interests. But do you bring news of the blessed Eugnostos?"

"Madam, Master Eugnostos has engaged me to deliver something to the hand of Nural Din the Andalusian."

"Then let us see what it is."

"I am sorry, my lady, but I may give it to him alone."

At this she laughed. "Dear Eugnostos! He has not lost his humor. Forgive me. I am Nural Din, physician of these estates, at your service." She looked at me carefully, and a smile crossed her lips. "So old Eugnostos has sent me an eagle. I am pleased you have come. Fold your wings awhile, and such accommodations as we have are yours."

"Thank you for your kindness, my lady," I said, "but I am merely a courier, assigned to procure and bring you this." So saying, I produced from within my cloak the ebony box. "With it comes a saying, but I know not its purport."

"What then is the saying, Magnalucius?" she asked, taking the box.

"Only this: *Find the Thinker, not the thought. Behold the treasure men have sought.*"

"*Find the Thinker, not the thought,*" she murmured. "But some messages are for the messenger, are they not?" Before she could explain we were interrupted by a turbaned Moor announcing dinner. Nothing more was spoken of my errand while we ate. That night I slept, somewhat uneasily, in a great canopied bed.

March the 11th

 Summoned to Nural Din's study at midmorning. "Now let us see what you have brought," she said, and producing the ebony box, she split the waxen seal with which I had secured the lid. Inside lay the precious sphere.

"Behold the Hesed! I knew Eugnostos would someday find it." Her voice was soft, but her eyes gleamed. She lifted the Peridam up into the slanting rays of the sun. "We move along in our mundane lives like leaves drifting down a river, barely aware of the turbulent depths below. Then inexplicably, we are pulled beneath the surface, and find ourselves moving with the great and unseen currents that rule the world above." She placed the box on her desk and picked up a clasp of copper wire. "And thus—" she deftly fitted the limpid sphere within its loops "—we are united with our destiny."

Then she turned to me. "*Preparato nos ab veritate.* In the name of holy mysteries I greet you. *The dragon is neither monstrosity, nor chimera, nor a creature of the imagination. It is revelation, a vehicle for truths that may not be cast simply in the static mold of words.*"

"*The Dragon?*" said I.

"Magnalucius," she said, "were you not told? We are hunting dragons."

Dragons? The woman was serious, of this there was no doubt. I felt lightheaded. The blessed Unicorn had once touched my life, a unique benediction. But dragons? Then why not centaurs and cyclopes and sphinxes prowling every mountain pass? Any educated man knew that such were mostly the concoctions of storytellers from old. *Dragons?* I looked to Nural Din for a sign that this was a riddle, yet her look did not waver. Dimly then arose a memory of a cold, commanding voice. A dragon? *A dream?*

"Magnalucius?" she asked.

"I was hunting the dragon, my lady."

"Then hear this story. It is an ancient tale from the *Dräg Edda*, and though much of it has been lost, what remains bears the stamp of truth, as such tales oftentimes do.

"Long long ago in the dim and dawning years, there was a hero named Otha Bréwulf, an Allemani of the Northern Forests. He was a hunter, the mightiest of all the Northmen, skilled in woodcraft and high in valor. He gathered to him a band of hunters, and together they roamed the great Black Forests, and slew Snagfir the wolf, and Urbu the bear, and the great wild ox. And though he had home and hearth and warm-armed wife, Bréwulf was unstill of spirit. He conceived a deadly wish to spear a Worm and claim its golden hoard. Then he learnt the crossing skills and with his men slipped the twilight

gate into the Dragon haunts, which are called the Magh Dá Cheo, the Plain of Two Mists, part of the Timeless Realm you may have heard named Brocileande.

"They spied the Serpent Unghirith and hunted her, and so great was their art that Unghirith, whose eyes were sharper than the hawk's, never saw her doom approach. They laid a snare and fell upon her with brazen spears as cold as morning, and pierced her brain. Then finding that her treasure lay in a bottomless pit beyond their reach, Bréwulf swore that in its stead he would bring home her head. Cursing, he hewed it off, flensed its scaly flesh, and tied it on a litter.

"But search as they would, they could not make passage back to their familiar lands, for it is the law of The Plain that no one may bring back the things that are native there.

"Thus wandered this unhappy band, sorely tried by hunger and homesickness, until the men pleaded with their captain to abandon his trophy. But he would not relent, and in anger they rebelled, and fought, and Bréwulf the Brave was slain. Then sorrow overcame the crew, and hanging the Dragonskull within a cave, they bore the body of their fairhaired chief away back to his wife and child.

"That is the story of Bréwulf as was told to me." She paused in the account. I saw the Moorish servant had silently entered the room and was listening carefully. "Now the story of his doomed and daring exploit was soon a matter of song, and rumors of the Dragonskull spread far until they reached the ears of Chú the Fomorian, who was the mightiest Druid of that time, and his seat was a hill far away on the shores of the Western Sea. A desire for that trophy burned in Chú's breast, and he turned all his thoughts to the lore of The Plain. Chú was a nightwalker and a rule-bender, and he marshaled Elementals from secret places and bound them to his will. He donned his badger headpiece with dangling claws and crossed into the Timeless Realm. He found the mighty skull, and pried two teeth from out of the thing. Concealing them in a gray oxhide painted with many spells, he burrowed past the twilight gate, and returning to our foursquare world he heaved his prize intact upon the ground.

"Then the Druid's hill groaned and sank from the burden of the Teeth, so that the forest around was washed beneath the sea, and his place was rendered as an island. This because the Law of The Worlds was broken. How much sorrow and mischief have come down to man

over the years from The Stealing of the Teeth! Yea, Magnalucius, even unto the woes of our own days.

"Chú girded his isle and ingathered his strength and contemplated long and deep the powers of his prize. He kindled his forges and hilted up both fangs with grips of bronze: one he decorated with red carnelians, the other with milk-pale pearls, and they were called the Red Dragon and the White. Then priests and wonderworkers flocked to his isle. Chú's fame spread across the land, and his deeds were both dangerous and sublime. But he was a lawbreaker. He had handled the naked teeth too much, and they broke his mind. In the end he flung himself into the raging sea and drowned.

"Then the Teeth of Unghirith fell into the possession of Iolo Oloi the oracle, his son and heir. His heart was free of scheming, for he knew the Unicorn, and there had come into his possession three mighty Periadams from the lands of Outremer. The greatest was *Assalam the Ruler*, and it is today in the keeping of Eugnostos. The other two, though lesser, were still of surpassing virtue: *Hesed* and *Hevurah*, the twins. Perceiving the raw and dangerous nature of the naked Dragontooth, Iolo wedded a Periadam to each fang with a golden clasp. Thus were opposites joined, and the dragonish force was tamed and something altogether new came into being.

"But alas, it was in Iolo's days that the seals of secrecy woven by his father were loosened. Word of the Dragonteeth traveled far and came at last to the ears of Fréwulf, grandson of Bréwulf, and he swore an oath to steal the things, for he accounted them as heirlooms of his house and people.

"Then begins a lay known as *The Flight of Guindal*, how Fréwulf and his shield-sister Guindal went to Iolo's isle, and while he made a lair on the wooded shore nearby, she arranged to be seemingly cast up upon the strand beneath Iolo's keep after a storm. Iolo found her there, fair and helpless, as the survivor of some dreadful shipwreck. Then by strategies she won his trust, and thus discovered the secret place where the teeth were kept. Then on a day when Iolo sojourned in his secret gardens, she gained the hidden chamber. The white Tooth was there but the red was not, and fearing that she would find no other chance, she seized the one and fled with her brother back to their dark lands. So they leave our tale and our thoughts, for your concerns are with Iolo and the tooth not taken."

"My concerns?" I cried, startled to find myself entering this ancient tale.

Nural Din held up her hand. "It was the Redfang that remained. Iolo soon learned that its mate had been carried into the fastness of the Northern forests. But he did not pursue the thing, for he was far-sighted, and saw that his destiny lay only with the one. The Redfang remained in the keeping of Iolo and his line for many generations, and each Holder kept watch over the land, and used its virtues secretly. But it is a restless thing and moved about until it disappeared out of histories and became a thing of rumor only, and then forgotten. Somewhere in this spread of years, the Periadam known as Hesed was separated from the Dragontooth, and Redfang's hard and ancient spirit rose up again with a surpassing vigor. The dragon is a brooding spirit, Magnalucius. He dissects everything with his cold and heartless mind. He worships beauty but comprehends it not. And even as we speak, *this tooth sits and spins threads of discontent everywhere about the kingdoms of the West.*

"When Redfang was split from its ruling sphere and where it lies now we do not know, for the Gnostic Brotherhood, who should have had a hand in these affairs, was lost in meditations while the mischief was being done. Yet the tale is not all bleak, for the Periadam has now returned."

So saying, she found a leather cord and threaded it through the amulet's clasp. "Hesed the Toothtamer is now recovered. If the Perilous Tooth were found, the two could be joined again, and the Healings would begin. This is the undertaking."

"Ah," I cried, the whole matter becoming (I thought) clear. "How may I aid you in this search?"

She shook her head. "It is not given me to bear this task. But there is another to undertake the Quest. One who procured the jewel, who knows the Timeless Land and whose heart is bound to service. And now that this one knows the Quest," she paused and lifted the amulet between us, her eyes holding mine, "will he take it?"

We both sat motionless there in her study. Behind her, motes of dust drifted weightless in the morning sunlight. Ah! One day (how long ago?), as a simple youth gazing at such a beam *I forgot myself,* and became as another speck of dust. How effortlessly I had floated in a vast and brilliant sea of light! It was the simplest sort of miracle, but the pure and simple peace of that moment has been my guide through all the intervening years. Now I was being offered seemingly the very opposite—danger and high drama. What was my course? But even as I pondered thus, my head inclined toward the amulet as if guided by another will, and Nural Din set the shining sphere around my neck.

"*Magnalucius Quester* you now shall be."

"Where does the search begin?" I asked.

"Perhaps you should begin here, and learn about the Dragon and the Tooth, and Druids as well." She went to her desk and withdrew a tattered binder. "Here," she said, opening it, "I have a picture of the thing." To my wonder, the motion loosened the very sheet to which she had referred, and a woodcut of the tooth fluttered like a homing pigeon to my feet.

"See how this thing seeks you out!" cried Nural Din. She immediately gave it to me. "I have carried this picture for many years. It came to me in England, where I sojourned after the Spanish expulsion. I practiced medicine in village and town there for whatever I could get. One day a wretch was brought to me whose hand had been hewn off. He was more dead than alive, but I nursed him back to vigor. He was penniless but prideful, and insisted on paying me with this picture, saying it was the only thing of value that he had, but worth more than gold. More than that he refused to say."

March the 12th

Nural Din's Moor (his name is Ibn Sufa) bid me join his mistress for breakfast in her study. Thus I commenced my research over coddled eggs in silver cups. I began with the Druid. At hand were mostly classical sources—the usual imaginative depictions with which the ancients excelled when they had little real knowledge of a subject. Diodorus claims the Druids are *philosophers and theologians, skilled in the divine nature, and able to communicate with the gods.* Then Tacitus claims the British Druids deemed it *a duty to cover their altars with the blood of captives and consult their deities through human entrails.* But wait. Hippolytus of Alexandria tells us that the Druids have *profoundly examined the Pythagorean faith!* A widely talented tribe, if all these stories are true! That they were formidable folk alone is certain.

Then, as light was waning, Nural Din led me to an ebony cabinet and unlocked its doors. Imagine my pleasure to find within a collection of books and scrolls all given to the subject of the Dragon! Of the titles the only one I recognized was the lost *Sigillum Dei Dragonis* of questionable authorship.

"Extraordinary!" said I. "Many of the manuscripts are originals, are they not? How did you assemble such a collection?"

She laid her hand on the polished wood. "Did you ever meet Valentinius of the Collegium?"

"He came and went before my time," said I, "though in the old days I sometimes heard his name."

"I likewise. Valentinius was that rarest of creatures, a spiritual genius, but troubled with an erratic nature. He would master a doctrine in the time it took other men just to hear it, then move to another. He knew the intricacies of the Kabbala, the protocols of alchemy—he passed through the Collegium like a comet; some thought he was a co-equal of Eugnostos. His mind seized upon the Dragon, and in his mercurial fashion, he accumulated this magnificent collection. Then, unaccountably, he disappeared, no one knows where. David of Leeds became Guardian of the Dragonlore, then myself, as you see."

"And Valentinius?"

She shrugged. "What path he followed only God knows. He would be be an old man today."

Tomorrow, then, *dragons*.

March the 13th

Every day now I follow Nural Din into the library and we swim like fish in its secrets. The Dragon (together with the Unicorn) is like a secret theme through time, surfacing like a chimera, touching the lives of the great, then disappearing. Here, the renowned scholar Abelard: *O masters of debate who would test the perfection of thy art,*

De Libro Nemeseos

Per annos claros et multos saeculi primi, Unicornes et homines condebant ita ut utraque genera crescerent in corporis animique statura

Sed alia nata erant in tenebris, et in tenebris convalescebant.

De Draconis Generatione

In illa die qua effecit Unicornis torrentem haec fontem e saxo sterili, gemina damnationis eiusque spatia sunt. Et singulam aquae illae fucentes se dispergerent longe lateque in terras secandas, primo cucurrerunt per ruinas obscuras sed illapsae in antra ardentia occultata circa mortuum radices. In illis antris profundis, expedit se illa prima vis Deificans in creaturam dira subledanda.

Ignis et Aqua

In hoc modo natus est draco, in cuius natura videmus testimonium generationis eius difficilis. Et numquam postea amplectetur illa creatura eandem vim et intelligentiam.

Draco primus vocabatur Yaldabaoth seu ita vocatur Iammas, et illi sunt multa alia nomina praeterea]

engage the Dragon! For he is mightily skilled in logic and rhetoric and all the arts of disputation. But beware! For though his intellect is vast, he has no heart. If thee best him, he is honorable, but you will pay dearly for any flaw in thought, even unto your life. . . . These accounts reach back, and back, even unto the very Beginnings. How different is this history, the Dragon and the Unicorn intertwining as twin threads on the loom of time.

I have decided to distill from all the diverse sources here a consistent narrative. Nural Din has sent Ibn this morning to a bookbinder to procure a journal suitable for this work. The work shall be called *The Book of Nemesis*.

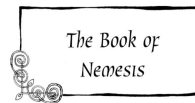

The Book of Nemesis

IN THE LONG, BRIGHT years of the First Age, Man and Unicorn dwelt together, and both races grew in stature of body and mind. But other beings had been spawned in darkness, and in darkness grew strong.

The Spawning of the Dragons

ON THAT VERY DAY when the Unicorn drew forth from barren rock a gushing spring of life, the seeds of doom were sown as well. For even as those shining waters spread their fertile moisture, they poured into unlighted fissures and trickled down to secret, burning caverns that wound among the mountains' roots.

There, in those abysmal chambers, the sacred waters' life-bestowing charge was first expended in raising up a living thing. And thus in fire and in darkness was the Dragon born. Her nature bears everlasting testimony to that uneasy birth, and ever after, no other creature has possessed the same measure of strength and cunning.

Now the first dragon was Yaldabaoth (though she is called Tliamat as well, and many other names besides). She was fearsomely wrought, with darting, lidless eyes; and the first sight caught in her unblinking gaze was her own image, reflected in the dark waters. She worshipped the sight, and a secret lust for that selfsame image has consumed her heart for all time since.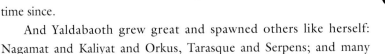

And Yaldabaoth grew great and spawned others like herself: Nagamat and Kaliyat and Orkus, Tarasque and Serpens; and many more besides. Now while dragons are of many sizes and shapes, all are swift and sharp of intellect, and thirst after knowledge. While the Unicorn seeks to divine the secrets of creation that he may more perfectly know the Creator, the Dragon desires the same that it may gain dominion over all the world, and thereby conquer death.

 Now the Dragon fiercely hates the Unicorn for his primacy, because it is not self-created, but owes to him its being. And so it has ever been the bane of the Unicorn, its fixed intent being to devour him, that it may no longer be an aftercomer, but be Oldest of All Things.

Now the Unicorn oversees all dominions of this world, and so in shadows and in fading light he finally must confront the Worm. No creature exceeds the Unicorn in quickness or in courage, but vast and subtle is the knowledge of the Dragon. It can mold its mind to his and lure him into the mazes of its thought, where the Unicorn tarries, judging that such intelligence cannot be utterly without redemption. And so, by imperceptible degrees is he lead into a debate unending; while the Dragon drains him of his strength and light. In those sunless halls his doom approaches; and only when he treads paths of thought that utterly violate his nature does he realize how grim his plight has become.

Then must the Unicorn traverse a narrow path. On the one side waits hatred; on the other, cold despair. Either will prove his defeat; for to succumb to hate would be to grasp his enemy's own device and perish in its fire. Yet if he flees, despairing and depleted, then will he be overtaken, be undone, and perish.

Meshed in confusion, the Unicorn knows for the first time the cold touch of the fear suffered by mortal men; the only fear that he shall ever know. But if he be steadfast, victory may still be claimed. With great sagacity, with highest love, *he must awaken as from a dream and, without hesitation, pierce the Dragon with his Spiral Horn.*

The Coming of Serpens The Deceiver

[*On the verso of same sheet, not shown:*]

BUT YALDABAOTH AND HER offspring brooded in vast vaults beneath the earth, and ever grew more jealous until at last they sent forth Serpens, the most cunning of their number. In size, it was minor

De mundi transformatione

Malis ergo cogitationibus hominum nunc se aptavit. Paulos-
dum viderent factus est mundi vernalis, paulatim obscurus
et asper. Super mentes eorum, venerant tenebrae.
Erant in illo tempore illi qui in vacuum et inane
inciderint.

Tenebrae deinde dissipatae sunt — ecce primo saeculo exres-
serant et tale regnum habebant, quale ante noverant, sed
regnum novum erat ambiguum et dissimile somni antiquo hominum.
Per dies viderunt diffidenter, quia regnum novum iam erat
tenuior trinus altius et homine erant, erant minus subtiles. Ex
illo tempore incipit saeculum argenteum generis hominum, Aetas
secunda.

Congeneres Crissi

Non mihi est propositum, et longum sit, narrare per singula
res gestas per aetatem secundam — non dicam, quam, asperam
fuisse viam hominibus optatam per trinam, fuerit ut genus
nostrum in hoc aditum, et ultimum saeculum. Unum
tantum dicendum — per omnes dies illas, Unicornis et
homo magisque vias dissimiles persecuti sunt. Tale
fuerat consilium Serpentis et sociorum illius.

Homines optabant residentia huius mundi ad domina-
tionem exercendam, et colebant idola et sculptilia,
et inter se debellabant, et in dies veniebant
sub mutila somnii cuiusdam fatalis. Tunc aliam viam
elegit Unicornis, quando homines manebant in-
corrigibiles in sua mala — non tam intermiscebant
pacem, generis quondam amicissima.

Sed nunc, quamdiu in regni tutela huius
domus, quam possidet Unicornis, cor eius tamen
dure ac acriter hominibus ligatum est.
Iterum tradit Unicornus viam erat per
fines terrarum nostrarum, cum tam morte
sibi, ita ut etias nunc Unicornem, ducius
erat, homo fortasse moveret summodo se ledet
ab eius torpore.

and so struck no fear in the hearts of men. Rather they thought the  Dragon comely and wondrous, for its scales were fiery and of all hues, and its words were finely chosen; and soon it was moving among Man as one familiar, clouding its purpose, as is the Dragon's craft. That is, it interwove words of praise with ones of doubt, saying, "What a wise and worthy ruler Man might have been!" and its every discourse lamented that the Unicorn should restrain his friends within the Garden.

Not all our race heeded these subtle lures of pride and discontent. Even from the first days, male and female were allotted their different intuitions; and so women were not deluded by Serpens' guile, but retained trust in their hearts, loving the Unicorn no less. But when at last Serpens heard men grumble that the Unicorn might be a less than perfect friend and bent instead on selfish wiles, then it spoke more openly. Beyond the Garden, the Dragon claimed, lay lands both fair and ripe for Man's dominion—a legacy denied him by the Unicorn, who held Man captive lest he grow too numerous to govern.

Now these lies did not escape the notice of the Unicorn, who walked in sorrow, and alone. For he could not compel Man to the paths of light, but only point the way; and in the debates of their untempered wisdom, no men sought his counsel. And of these, the most deluded rose up, crying, "Let us break our golden chains and bid farewell to bondage! And if the longer, harder path we choose, far brighter shall the ending be!"

 Thereafter, for all the ills and sorrows that would befall, men could not blame any but themselves. For the rest cried out in loud approval, even as the women bowed their heads in grief. And thus the Dragon's work was done, and so these words became the doom of Man.

On the Changing of the Age

THEN MOVED THE HOLY ONE, in perfect accord with Man's ill-conceived intents. And within the hour, the springtime world grew hard and dim. And it seemed that forgetful emptiness descended on men's minds, and when that darkness was lifted up, behold, they found themselves in a denser realm, a shadow of their former one. Uncertainly at first they moved, being clad in coarser form. And from that hour was counted the beginnings of the Second Age, called the Age of Silver.

The Sundering of the Kindred Races

NOW IT IS NOT WITHIN my compass to chronicle each age, nor the bitter path that led Man to this fourth and final world. Only this needs be said: that Man fell into a moral slumber, worshipping idols and fighting against his neighbor. And through all these afteryears, Man and Unicorn grew ever more apart, as Yaldabaoth and her kind had wished.

Then did the Unicorn go upon his separate way while Man stood firm in folly, and thus their mingling was at an end. But while the Garden of that golden realm remains his rightful home, the creature's heart is still bound to Man, and so ever he travels across the sundry worlds to linger at our present boundaries.

And even now may a man meet the Guide, if he but waken from that fretful sleep [of error].

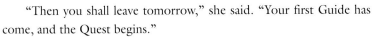

March the 18th

Today a restless energy rose within me and I brought *The Book of Nemesis* to a close. I told Nural Din.

"Then you shall leave tomorrow," she said. "Your first Guide has come, and the Quest begins."

"What guide is this?"

"*Urgency.* Without urgency there is no quest. Set your sails, it will carry you out of the harbor."

"But where am I to go?"

"Simply complete each step of your journey; the next will show itself."

"I do not understand," said I.

"Are you not going to visit your esteemed brother?"

"But surely he cannot aid me."

"No matter, forge ahead," said Nural Din. "I will send with you Ibn Sufa as aide and companion. He is steadfast and as good a friend as you might hope for, for he has traveled too, and has knowledge of many things."

May Almighty God be the Doer and the Beneficiary of this endeavor. With all my reservations, my heart is quickened by the prospect of what lies before me.

March the 19th

Parted from Nural Din of Andalusia at sunrise. As we stood on the threshold of the villa, my good host's smile dropped and she took on a solemn mien. "The Periadam you carry is a living link with the Dragontooth, and will draw to you the three Guides: Urgency, Wisdom, and Surrender." She turned to her servant. "Ibn, most trustworthy of men, I cannot now give you freedom, for yours is already the freedom that cannot be bestowed. But in undertaking this journey your debt is erased forever. *He who is the greater is the servant of the other.*"

Thus we parted. I confess my heart, as the poets say, leapt to meet the road. I set out to meet my noble step-brother, but who could hazard what marvels lay beyond? I felt as if all my parts had come together in a noble and proper compounding.

I see that Ibn Sufa is a man of competence, having lashed a great load of gear onto a pack mule, and saddling our horses, all before dawn.

(Preceding page missing, no date)

The place where ——— is now established was not far, being a manor-house in this same estate set like a jewel overlooking a shallow and meandering river. As we rode up, the bright morning sun shone on a vast bed of early blooming daffodils. I prayed that here my brother had found a suitable home. We were received most cordially by a bustling servant and shown to ———'s rooms where we embraced each other joyfully. He looked like a prophet of old, and though all the days of his troubled life were graven upon his face, his mind was as agile as ever. He showed great interest in my notes and drawings, but nothing in his apartments gave any indication of what might now be his concerns. Yet throughout our conversation, the familiar majesty of his intellect was tempered by the melancholy which perenially lay about his soul. He had ceased (as had been his wont) to use the few

years of age he has on me to play the master; the only vestige of that vexing habit being a most brotherly concern about my affairs. The interview ended most amicably, and his servant Giovan showed us to lovely quarters overlooking the river.

Nural Din came today to examine ———'s arm, which has turned quite numb (though he kept the malady concealed from me yesterday). Ibn and I took the opportunity to explore the countryside, and rested at a small inn. Royal company was rumored nearby and the place was bustling. But my brother's name was a charm, and we were shown to a quiet alcove, where I found journal and pen. I could not help but notice a handsome youth seated nearby. He was wearing a black velvet cloak, but his clothes underneath had the angular cut of German fashion. He seemed to be examining a large map. I rarely accost strangers, but my curiosity was aroused, so I rose to introduce myself. But as I approached his table, he rolled up his map, and addressed me. "Good sir, you seem familiar," he said. "Have our paths crossed before? In Parma perhaps?" I nodded that I had recently passed that way. "No matter! Would you join me now? It is uncommon to see someone writing in a rustic inn. What is your occupation that you sit here on an afternoon occupied in letters?"

"I keep a journal," I said, "—only a few observations of the countryside."

"How interesting," he exclaimed. "And what have you discovered?"

"Scenery changes, but people are everywhere the same."

"Yes," he answered, "that is true enough. But am I mistaken, or are you not like myself an artist? You have the air of one who sees past appearances. Please excuse me, may I introduce myself? My name is Johann and I am traveling to broaden my perspective. Perhaps we could compare our work sometime." He poured two glasses of wine, then drawing out a bejeweled dagger, he stirred mine with its tip, and handed it to me. "*Endegut, allesgut, allesgut, endegut,*" he said, then seeing my expression, laughed. "Oh this? It is an old custom of my countrymen."

At that moment, my new manservant appeared at the table with news that my mare had a sudden croup, and that I should have a look at her. Knowing the animal was quite fit, I nevertheless excused myself and followed him out to the stables. There he turned to me with a look of concern. "You must guard yourself, my lord. Something about that fellow was not right."

"Why do you say so?" I asked, annoyed at the effrontery of his intervention.

He shrugged, and lowered his lids. "Only a feeling, my lord."

I let the matter drop, and we departed. Perhaps the good fellow was confirming something troubling that I myself felt. I suspect the matter has not yet run its course.

March the 21st

Met again with my dear brother in the fore-noon. He said he wished to share some of his thoughts. Then, to my surprise, he ceased his far-ranging discourse and in the most candid way revealed to me his fears of death. His sincerity was affecting, and soon I confessed to him what was occupying my own mind, finishing with an account of yesterday's odd encounter in the inn. He listened with the greatest attention to every detail, and stroked his beard a long time in silence. I waited for him to dismiss my quest as an antique fairy tale.

"Have you ever heard of the line of Lost Kings?" he said at last.
"Never."

He turned and disappeared into his inner apartments. The sun had dipped to the horizon when he emerged with a hand-lettered page in his hand.

"It is just as well," he said (as if he had only just left the room). "At long last it may be that I have some scrap of knowledge that may give you aid." He handed me the sheet. It was fairly new, no doubt a copy of an older original.

"Read on," he said. "And you may keep it."

Prince Ursus

In the dark years after the Fall of Rome, there was a Scambrian prince named Ursus, descended from the most noble kings of Christen–dom. Ancient treachery had denied him his throne, and in his powerlessness, Prince Ursus called to him all who might have counsel, both ministers and thieves. Many came, for he was well-loved, and they debated and made many suggestions, but none offered hope.

Then a scullery-crone who had served the house for generations came forth, and she said that a house has many tales, and years ago one had come to her ears that now might help her lord.

This was the tale: A distant forebear in the Prince's line was exiled as a child to the land of Fodla. There he grew to manhood and wed a Celtic princess. This was in the Year of our Lord 666, which was accounted strange, for that is the number of the Antichrist. She had in her dowry a great enchanted Tooth, but the Prince swore that if she was to join with him she must abandon this talisman, for he was a Christian, and abjured all pagan things. Loving him, she left the Tooth in the safekeeping of the monastery where he had been raised and schooled.

Upon hearing this tale, Prince Ursus sent a trusted knight to regain the talisman as his inheritance. Against all hope it was brought to him, and wielding it he rose in force to regain his land and kingship. But he was betrayed by the Tooth, for he was not privy to its secrets, and he fell into defeat and was banished. Then in bitter anger Prince Ursus buried the Tooth under a mighty Longstone in the land of his exile, where it lies still.

"But this must be the same Perilous Tooth!" I cried.

"That is what I thought," said my good brother, "but I know not whether it is wise for you to join in this hunt. I wonder if this Dragontooth you seek has a spirit imprisoned within, such as did the famous ring of Lorenzo di Medici? Instead of hunting talismans, should you not retire to a lonely place and practice the meditations you have acquired?"

He became distracted and fell silent. Rubbing his arm, he retired.

I rarely dream. That night I did. I saw a man in royal dress, whom I took as Prince Ursus. He had a great tooth in one hand, a shovel in the other, and he wandered here and there over a muddled landscape. Then the dream turned clear and every detail vivid. Wild jagged cliffs crowned with mist loomed up, the Prince was gone, and before me stood a frail and wizened man in long white robes. He wore a hoop of twisted gold about his neck. He motioned me to step closer.

"O Magnalucius! I have walked these paths before you. I Nemthenga also sought the awful Orm-tooth, hero's ruin, bane of nations. Now let my sorrows save you heartache. This is a most unwise errand; the thing you seek brings only doom and ruin! If a master's judgment falters, a noble caution befits the moment. Seek the lights of heaven! Let the Dragontooth lie in its own darkness.

How soft and reasonable was his voice! His words roused hidden doubts, and I reached out and touched his hand to see if he were real. But his flesh was cold and I recoiled, grasping at the Periadam which hung at my breast. *In Nominea Dios!* I cried in a loud voice, and then, *Where did Ursus hide the Tooth?* The old man's eyes widened in fear, and he moved his lips as if being forced to speak, but the only sound he could make was a strange choking gasp: *errgrahhh.* . . . I awoke in fear.

The dream stayed with me all the next day. Had I visited the Plain, the Magh Dá Cheo? Who was the priest? I recounted the dream at dinner to ———. He chewed thoughtfully the whole time, and said nothing.

March the 22nd

 This morning ——— knocked as I was completing yesterday's entry in this journal. The windows were thrown open and the heady smell of roses filled the room.

"Three things," he said. "*Primero*: The story of Prince Ursus revealed the land where your debatable Tooth is buried, and I will tell you where it is. *Segundo*: Your dream is a portent, but I cannot read it. Find one who can. And I would counsel you to travel without delay, indeed to leave before cockcrow, because, *Tercero*: There is one now likewise searching for this Perilous Tooth who should not find it."

"The one who murdered Severinus?" said I.

"Possibly. I speak of the man in the inn. It is Master Faust of Thuringia, the Kabbalist, of course. Do not let his youth deceive you. I am told he is most accomplished in the alchemical arts, both light and dark, and your suspicions are undoubtedly well-founded. He is ambitious and I am sure he too is seeking this talisman, and hopes to learn from you its whereabouts."

"But I do not yet know where it is!" I cried.

"No matter," said he. "You know much. He seeks to make your acquaintance, to glean the content of your journals. Discerning your next destination, he would dart ahead to obtain the prize! Even if he can retrace your path he gains much, for then he can learn what you have learned. It is best to regard him as your adversary. And others may appear, drawn like flies to the power of this legendary tooth. Sweet brother! How have you wandered into such a dangerous intrigue as this?"

"And how is it that you are so informed on these arcane matters?" I asked.

"Magnalucius," he said, "I have been many places and seen many things. Do not be surprised that I too know something of such mysteries."

"Do you advise that I destroy my journals then?"

He took on a pained expression. "No, no, they are a part of you. Who knows? Some jotted detail, easily forgot, could later prove to be the crucial element in this search. Do this: firstly, strike my name from your notes. Then, I know an admirable code which. . ." He paused. "No, you would not hold to it. Here: simply obscure the placenames where you have visited, and do not commit to writing such details henceforth. This will hide your trail from thieving eyes."

March the 23rd

We parted outside the manor chapel where he had been at prayer. "I shall not be up to see you depart," he said, "for I have never taken to your monkish hours. Farewell now, and let there only be love between us, for we may not meet again."

"There is a bond between us never to be broken," I said. "Do you remember the secret cave you showed me when we were children in the Appenine?" He smiled. Then taking his hand I asked, "Brother, is there an errand I may perform for you?"

He hesitated. "There is. I have a new interest now." He lifted the rosary he was fingering. "O fear not, Chipolinno, the irony does not escape me. I shall not become a *penitente* in black. The Church is still intrigue and pride and empty pomp, but beneath I detect a miraculous light, like the moon on a stormy night: now seen, now obscured, but always there above the tumult. Thus I have conceived a wish to see a cathedral said to be the most sublime expression of faith ever made. But my traveling days are over. Before you disappear into your quest, go there in my place and write to me of what you see!"

Old ways die hard. He was (without realizing it I am sure) testing to see if I knew the place. I skirted the trap. "Willingly," said I. "I would only ask that you provide my Moor with traveling instructions, for I am told he knows the land better than many a native-born."

"I will provide him every instruction for a speedy journey. Thank you, brother."

"May Christ King increase your days and reveal to you his kingdom," I said. "I will ask a blessing for you at this holy place." Thus we embraced and parted without contention and I account this not the least of miracles. Tomorrow we shall leave before cockcrow.

A Letter

Dear Brother,

Thank you for sending me to this marvelous place! I thought I was prepared for the sight, for in my stays at the Collegium I often visited the nearby old church of San Francisco, designed (it was said) by the Saint's own companion Elias. There I saw the intention, but here! Perfection. One steps into another world. A gasp, a vertigo: everything rushes upward to infinity! A choice is offered—resist or surrender. Ah, but plunging in, one joins with such lofty thoughts. Yes, your tales were true. Here is a place made by angels, not by men! The light! The soaring space! Such designs, rendered in windows of colored glass, wherein our solid stony world is fragmented, dissolved and reborn as higher substance. Perhaps you have heard these things before. At first I thought it was all that I had come to see. Yet as I marveled, my eyes finally lowered to my feet and I saw that I stood upon a curious maze set in colored stone. It was not decoration, but essence, for the builders had put it in the mystic center of the place. Thus I contemplated its secrets, and for an afternoon it rewarded me. I have copied it for you. See! Here is the Pilgrimage of Man from outer darkness to celestial inner light.

Whilst drawing the maze, an old mason came and joined in my communion. "They knew the Christian order would fail," he whispered, "and the master builders knew they could not fix Truth in words, for words would be corrupted. They chose stone, which time would not decay, to be read afresh by each generation in the language of the heart." How prettily said! He was learned in many things, even the dreamlore of the Sufis, so I put to him an account of my dream. He questioned me closely about the circumstances of my life, and so discovered where I am bound and the nature of my search. He laughed and revealed how my dream pointed to where it must be. How marvelous! Are we not caught up in a grand pattern? —M.

(Copy and send by common carrier.)

Ibn likewise is much taken with the church and maze. After dinner he asked what places on this venture I had visited before he took service with me. Hearing my brief account, he pondered a moment and said, "Then here be the sixth station of your quest."

"The sixth? How so?"

"Station the first—the very beginnings, your mother-birth. Station the second—you meet your master, he imparts to you the Undertaking. Station the third—finding the Hesed. And so onward until here." Clever Ibn. I had not thought of this mission like that, yet he has struck upon a truth. Tomorrow we set out for station seven. Onward!

April the 15th

How great my wonder at this stupendous work of the ancients! In these Standing Stones (which I never knew existed) is an achievement equal to the cathedral. But how different. They impart a more ancient longing of the soul which I am powerless to describe. One is drawn back to a Golden Age when men moved in harmony with powers that we have long forgot. A fitting place to hide a dragon's tooth. The countryside here is unremarkable and mostly uninhabited, but at one time it must have been well-populated. Though by what race? And what gods? Now to find which is the Longstone of Ursus.

In my week with Nural Din, Ibn had engaged a tailor from a nearby town to sew a gay and roomy tent, which he is now pitching outside the Stones.

Station VII
The Stone

April the 17th

We awoke today in a sea of drifting mist. Together Ibn and I walked among the ghostly stones. They seemed alive, awakened by priest-architects into rocky sentinels that lived and breathed. I feel them watching.

By mid-morning, the sun had dissolved the mist into tattered wisps, and a dark-haired young woman came, picking the artemesia and borage that grows about this place. She was intent on her work and spoke little. Ibn made her acquaintance, and spent some time assisting her search for a particular herb. Toward eventide, he returned to where I sat sketching. Her name is Lind, he said, and she knew the names of the stones. She knew the stone we sought and . . . [portion of MS. waterstained] . . . through the waving grass. Swarms of tiny

74

white-winged butterflies rose up before us. Finally Lind stopped and pointed at the great corpse of fallen stone half-buried in a mass of yellow jessamine and twining honeysuckle.

"How do you read it, Ibn?" I asked.

"A prince entombs a treasure beneath a standing, not a fallen stone," he said. "It was risen in the days of Ursus. I think he had a tunnel bored beneath it and there put the Tooth to rest."

"My thoughts as well. And then at a later time another came, threw down the stone and took the Tooth?" The unspoken was heavy in the air.

"My lord, I would say it was a mighty power that flung down that stone."

There it was. *What sort of man—if mortal man it was—did we now pursue?* Ibn and I returned to our tent, the girl to her hearth. That night I wandered under the stars. Where now?

April the 18th

Ibn came to me this afternoon, and wordlessly laid before me an artifact of corroded copper, still damp and flecked with clay.

"A snake," I said, "quite old, and crudely made."

"Or dragon?" said Ibn.

"Or a dragon!" said I, turning it over. "With an old coin as its eye. Where did you find this thing?"

"Thinking to search for some clue as to who felled the mighty stone and took the Tooth, I spent the morning rooting around its base. It was there that I found it. I hope it has a tale to tell."

A clever man; his copper find is now our only guide. There is much to Ibn Sufa al-Iskandaria. I cannot say I ever know his thoughts, but I am discovering that his selflessness is tempered with an independence of spirit. An ideal servant, one senses in him an utter lack of servility. Indeed he possesses a quality which I must call noble. Sometimes he seems almost amused with his status as servant, as if he knew that tomorrow he would awaken a prince. This place has its secrets too. It slows the flutterings of thought, and we are peaceful. We will stay another day.

Lind came again late in the day. Originally I had taken her for a peasant maid, for she was barefoot, with the vitality of folk who labor in the soil. Yet today the lace upon her smock spoke of a finer birth. She is not unattractive, and Ibn spent more time assisting her today. I shall warn him, for we are creatures of the road now, and dalliances ill befit us.

Eventide was falling and she was at her herbs, and singing some folk-air. It had an indescribable taste of sweet sadness, and I fell under its melodic spell. Then I saw glimmering in the half-light beyond the stones a solitary unicorn listening as well! It wheeled and leapt away, and left me trembling. So enchanting a vision! I am filled with certitude that success will crown this venture. What happy fate ordains that I should know both Unicorn and Dragon, the first being what all men seek, the other what all men fear? What must I learn from this blessing? That, though in utter opposition they are nonetheless connected? Or even that they are of the same inexplicable substance?

Nothing compels us to go, so we shall stay on.

"Ibn," said I this morning, "has our quest come to an end? We have watched, we have waited, we have found nothing but a copper snake. I would move on, but I know not where."

Mid-morning Ibn approached me, saying that the *forest friends* of Lind wished to meet us. We headed north on a well-worn trail, she leading on Mathias the pack mule. We rode several hours till we saw from afar a deep forest, but it was midday before we arrived under its mighty limbs. I took it to be a remnant of the great forests that once must have covered this fair country. It was mostly oak, and filled with vine and bramble where it met the fields. We dismounted and Lind led a way onto a narrow track that wound between the trees. At last we went up a low hill, and came to a solitary rock raised up, all girt with ivy, so that we could scarcely see its top. She motioned us to sit and began to play her sweet melancholy tune upon a wooden flute. Soon there emerged from the forest shadows a dozen of the most curious people I have ever seen. Their long hair swept over their shoulders, man and woman both; they were small and slight

XIV Kal. Mai.

Jhn mihi hodie post meridiem venit et coram me
sine verbo aliquando posuit, aliquid aeruginosum,
tam madidum et limo
tinctum. — Serpens?
in quam, perterritus

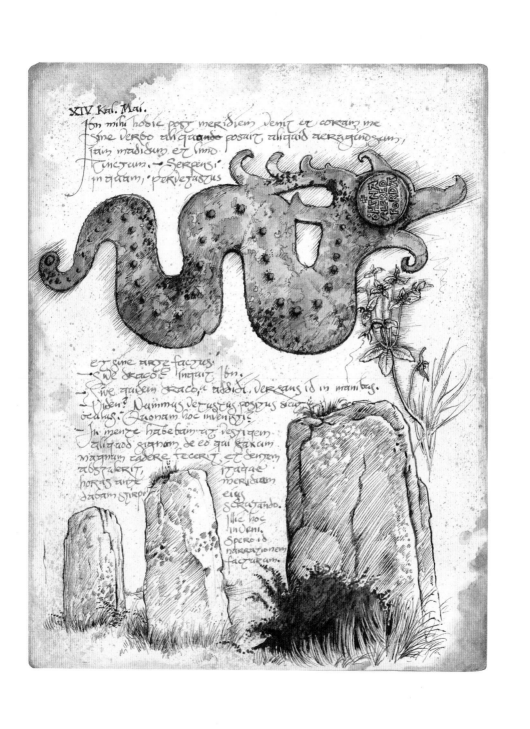

et sine arte factus?
— Sive draco. inquit Jhn.
— Sive quidem draco, addidi, vertens id in manibus.
— Viden? Nummus vetustus pospus sicut
oculus. Quonam hoc invenisti?
— In mente habebam ut vestigem
aliquod signum de eo qui saxum
magnum cadere fecerit, et denique
abstulerit,   itaque
horas ante   meridiem
dabam stirpi   eius
                        scrutando.
                        Ille hoc
                        inveni.
                        Spero id
                        narrationem
                        facturam.

in stature, not at all like the sturdy rustics hereabout. Their ankles were slim and they walked lightly, like cats. Their faces were happily proportioned, with large and shining eyes and intelligent foreheads. They crouched in a circle, swaying slightly with the music. When Lind ceased her playing they began to converse with her in musical voices and delicate gestures. Finally one turned to me, and spoke. Lind translated.

"O traveler from afar, how high the sea, how red the moon?"

"Do not be perplexed," said Lind. "This is the question they ask all guests. For when the sea rises, they say, and the moon turns red, their time has come again."

"Why do they not watch the sea themselves?" I asked.

"Oh no!" she cried, "The sea fills them with such longing they fear gazing upon it they would die."

"Good people," I said to them, "the sea and the moon remain as ever."

"It is their sadness," said Lind, "that in their leafy forest homes they cannot view the stars as once they did. Ever their numbers diminish, for their forest borders are hewn and plowed, and they know they have come to the twilight of their years. Alas for us, for there is much that we might learn from them. To their fate they are resigned, but someday they will raise their stones again and converse with the stars. They say:

> *We will return, walking again without fear.*
> *We will return, singing the West Wind up in our faces.*
> *Shining brightly we will return, like the moon, shining like*
>   *the moon,*
> *Always returning."*

"O traveler, what is your song and what do you carry?" said another.

Ibn motioned me to show the stone, and I moved my cloak so as to uncover the amulet. "Killina, Killina!" they cried. The oldest of them, a woman with gray-streaked hair came and knelt in front of me. Like a curious child, she reached out and touched my wrist, then my cheeks and forehead.

"You know the Friend?" she said. "Killina, too beautiful to be aware of imperfection, too innocent to know fear, too gentle to suspect violence." The others echoed her words after each statement.

"Killina is always standing nicely in his place, his little ears trembling." As she spoke her face became young and eager like the Unicorn's.

"Killina is a great hunter, shining like a ray of light for you!" Their eyes shone with delight.

I knew I was to speak, but I felt clumsy and my tongue was stilled. "Good folk," I finally said, "I seek your aid. I am searching for the Red Dragontooth. Have you knowledge of where it lies now? We are told that once it lay beneath the fallen stone."

One among them stood. "O friend of Killina. We saw the Tooth laid beneath the stone, we heard it went away. But we do not know where it has gone."

"Old Ones," said I. "Then my servant and I are lost, and we know not what to do."

A man with braided hair spoke up. "We say, *when in doubt, seek beginnings.*"

"Then where are the beginnings of the Tooth?"

An old woman wrapped in deerskin spoke. "We Old Ones know the terrible teeth, and where they were first brought. They came to the Ictis, the great gray rock. See, here is where it is." Then she pushed the litter of the forest floor aside, and shaped a map from the clay beneath. "All this is sea, and here and here is land, and here is the isle." The shadows of the forest had grown deep. "But beware, beware. Dragon is alive and everywhere." She twined an arm so convincingly that it became a serpent. "*Here is the dragon slinking round your heart,*" she said. "*Better to find this one, O traveler.*"

They all laughed. One of the elders lifted his head and began sniffing the air. As one, they quickly rose and disappeared back into the forest.

"The Old Ones," said Lind, when the last had gone. "Their songs recall the Age before the Flood. Once they sang on every hill, and named the stars, and raised their standing stones. Then came the wild Celts with spears of bronze and gods of war and took their standing stones. Rome came next, and the Old Ones faded into the trackless woods beyond the reach of plow and sword."

Ibn smiled at me in his obscure way. "An interesting folk, my lord?"

"Yes," I replied, "most interesting. Let us go."

This Moor Ibn has been with me now for long enough to take his measure, but some essential thing eludes me. He is some five and thirty years, his skin the color of dark polished oak, nose long and thin, hair cropped and wiry. There is a negligent grace about his movements, and the odd remark reveals an educated man. But his eyes: sometimes piercing like a hawk, more often abstracted or removed. But if one peers too deeply within, his lids drop like the curtains of the sultan's carriage. Perhaps he is indeed a prince upon his native soil. Yet he seems to derive pleasure from his duties, and performs even the most insignificant service cheerfully. An ideal traveling companion, for he is not given to idle chatter, and neither am I. Spent afternoon breaking camp. We are off to the Isle of Ictis!

Our captain was expert at catching the least breath of air in his patched sail, and he jibbed through drifting mists, always keeping within earshot of the slap of waves along the shore. That and the creak of the boom were the only sounds. Even the seabirds stayed in their nests. We sailed somewhere between heaven and earth in a nether-world without horizon. If a sea dragon had risen dripping from the deeps beside us, I would not have been surprised. Finally when the isle appeared, it was floating above us in the

Station VIII
The Dragonskull

firmament. "There it be," said our seaman softly, and swung his tiller. A small dock emerged from the whiteness. A seagull swooped low, mewing in the mist. *There is power here*, I thought, *it rolls around this isle like surf.* We gained the jetty and the captain's son made fast. Ibn heaved my cases ashore. "God grant your wishes," said the boy. I paid his father our passage, and a waiting fee, and they settled into their sailcloth cabin. If the next leg of our journey were to be by sea they would be here. Stone stairs climbed up the steep flanks of the isle through bracken and pine. High above, stone ramparts sprouted from the sides of the mount and disappeared into the mists. To one side, a noisome drainage ditch was cut

VII 18. Jun.

Gubernator noster peritus erat
ad auram ad hymam in velo eius resarto
capiandam, et per caligines ingrabiles
proram verzebat, semper audiens
undae ad litrus gonaer reb. Undae
gonantes et malus crepans gonus
nullus alrus. Aves maritimae in
nisli mandabant. Inter
zaelum et terram navigabamus, sine hora zonze sicut
in inferis.

CUM
BIODH

RATH

ILE DO

THURUS

AB
INSOMNI
NON
CVSTODITA
DRACONE

Draco de profundis
capat erigens
nort
mihi horrendum
fuerit.

into the hill. Another rocky path set off around the shore, a large stone cross standing where it plunged among massive boulders.

As we gathered up our things, we spied a friar striding down the path as if to meet us. He wore a coarse brown covering over a white habit, and had the sturdy bearing of one who does not shun toil. He helloed us in the native tongue, but I returned "Peace be with you!" in good high Latin.

"And may the peace of the blessed saints be with you!" he returned in the same tongue, coming up to us. "Welcome then to the Mount. Who be you, and from where are you come?"

"Two pilgrims, from the lands of Italy."

"Then follow me," said he, "and tell me a tale." He slung up the largest of my panniers, and marched up the path. The climb was dramatic, and Ibn and I arrived well-winded at an iron shod gateway that passed through the battlements. We continued up a spiral stair into a room of dressed stone. It once must have served as barracks for the postern guard, but now it was fitted with a bed, chest, and gilt Greek icon at one end, at the other, table and chairs. There was a warm hearth, and some kitchen gear. In one corner stood a sword.

"Now take some bread and share your trip with me," he said heartily. "We get few visitors this time of year."

He was a large man, but his features were fine, and his hands were graceful. From the lines on his face some three score years were behind him, but he wore them well.

"I am Magnalucius, this is my servant Ibn Sufa al-Iskandaria. I am a scholar of old histories, in search for ancient sites and stories."

"Here you have found both," said the monk, as he removed a large loaf of crusty brown bread from his cupboard. "In ancient days the Druids came and delivered their oracles. But the Gospel conquered and those cruel days are gone. And I beg you not deem me thoughtless for offering you only the waters of our spring, but that is what I have." So saying he poured us mugs of clear water.

"I have learnt my share of songs and tales," said the friar. "Now what histories do you seek?"

"I pursue a tale called the *Dräg Edda*. It has been said some part was played out upon this very rock."

He went to the recessed window and looked out into the muted evening light. "*Dräg Edda. Dräg Edda*. Indeed! A saga of the North. A history of Déowulf . . . or is it Bréwulf? How does it go? 'Got snorr ley dürr fon Ithsdon Horr.' Oh yes: a foolish tale, full of the wild imaginings of a morose people."

"But it is said that ancient tales sometimes hide a secret verity," I said. "How could they have persisted through the centuries without some nub of truth?"

"Truth no doubt, but truth for whom? It is, as I recall, full of dragons and talismans. A tale concocted by some bard to please his lord on a winter's night." He gave me a hard look, and judging that that explanation did not serve me, continued. "And at best were they not glimpses into a dark world where good Christian men would not want to venture?"

Did something in his voice lack conviction? Without thinking, I slipped my hand beneath my mantle to touch the Periadam that hung around my neck.

The man's head lifted at that moment, as a doe in the forest detecting a sound. "But then," he said, turning toward me, "what did you say your name was? Forgive me."

"I am called Magnalucius, of the Collegium Gnosticum."

"The Collegium Gnosticum?"

"An ancient order founded by the gnostic fathers. But yours? I do not recognize the habit you wear."

He sat up straighter. "I am Milesian, servant of God, bishop of the Celi Dé Reclaimers. The Dé occupied this place long before Saint Benedict was born, and in token of our primacy one of our line keeps eternal watch here on the Isle."

The Reclaimers of Celi Dé! The elusive Celtic monks of legend. I shifted my cloak so that the shining stone was uncovered.

He drew in a great breath of air and let it out slowly. "Well now," he said. "Do I see upon your breast a certain storied stone?"

"Milesian, I search Beginnings, for the ancient seat of Chú. The Edda has begun again."

He sat in silence. From outside, the rich tang of seawind drifted in the open window. "Here is that place," he said. "Here dark and sorcerous deeds were done."

"And great shining ones as well," said I.

He nodded. "Both. In that age we moved easily from the waking
world into the timeless realm and back again. That was the childhood
of our race, when, as they say, *the dragon strove with man.* But now the
lands have changed, and the Laws as well. *The cup is spilled, the halls
are laid to ruin.* Though I abide here on a remote hill, I am not igno-
rant of the restless tide now rising in the west. But tides may turn and
cups be filled and raised again." He rose suddenly and moved to the
door with almost a leap. "Do you wish to know more? Come!"

To Ibn, who had not moved, he said, "Friend, this is a journey
your lord must take alone. But here stay and be my honored guest. There are candle and
flint on that corner shelf, the *Philokalia* on the trunk, if you read Greek." So saying he
led me out the postern door and down the paths until we drew next to the stone cross,
and there he motioned me to lead. "Let us see what there is to see here," and he guided
me gently through the boulders with his hand upon my back. Then, as I stepped
between them, with an awful shove, he sent me careening forward. So ill-mannered and
surprising was this act that it took my breath away. The world turned dark and I believe I
swooned, though somehow I did not fall. Mind reeling, I gained my wits, and saw that I
stood no longer above a hissing sea, but in a craggy wilderness overlooking a shadowy
plain! The ramparts above us were gone; there was not the slightest sign of human habi-
tation. I turned in utmost confusion to my host, and he responded
with a look of grave intensity.

"Behold Magh Dá Cheo, the Plain of the Two Mists," he said.
"Follow, if you wish to know the beginnings."

I followed. The ground was moist, and a rich damp fragrance
filled the air. Wild mountains rose beyond the plain, and the sun hung
at the horizon just as in the world we had left behind us. My host
moved quickly forward down a narrow defile, for light was waning.
We threaded our way along a path between jagged outcroppings, all
overgrown in places with a rich cloak of fern and moss glowing like
jewels in the last golden rays of the sun. There seemed to be ancient
languages writ in the delicate wrinkles that adorned the rocks, but I
cannot say for sure. My spirit rose in gladness, for I had found my way
into the magic hidden realm!

Sine verbis mihi indicavit Milesius
ut eum intus sequar. Eius
gestus auspiciebam cautissime
semper, paratus ad insidias.
sed pedes eius retractavit
comiter.

Hic mandata mihi monstravit
aliquid magnum et con-
solatum, in tenebris sus-
pensum. Id spectavi
diu perplexus, donec
caput obscurum
id esse
discernere
possem,
monstravique
et de animali
studuimque cog-
nito. Frontem
eius in ex-
tergo cub-
itum hab-
uit, et
cornua
et dentes
magnae de
calvariis
erant.
Sed pulchra
guido eius erat
ferox et tamen
ordinata ad usum.
Ideo cognovi mente ibi
sine carne voluntatem
antiquam et cultam.
Mihi apparuit sicut
gladius micans
plenus rationis et
plenus
myst cerebri...

Before long I became aware of silent waves of energy beating upon me, as if I were a deaf man approaching a great cataract. Soon we came before an opening into the side of a cliff, and I knew that the source of this perturbation lay within. I did not feel afraid, but tense and eager. Wordlessly Milesian motioned for me to follow him inside. I eyed his movements carefully, suddenly aware of the possibilities of treachery, but he merely stepped aside.

The dying light illuminated a great and convoluted thing hanging in the darkness. A long moment I regarded it in puzzlement, until with a start I saw it was a monstrous skull unlike any creature that I knew. Its forehead was fully three spans in width, and armed with horns and tusks. Yet it was also a thing of fierce and efficient beauty, and I knew suddenly that though the flesh was gone a refined and ancient will remained. Like a shining sword, it was both supremely rational and mystical. It would accept no obstacle; it would penetrate every opposing strategy in pursuit of higher purpose.

My rush of insight was broken by Milesian's voice, echoing as if from a great distance: "Ecce Dragonis, Behold and beware!"

Beware? All cloudiness was banished from my mind, and for the first time I thought truly able (I felt) to see things as they really were, unobscured by human sentiment. Beyond doubt it was the simple proximity to this thing that so elevated my mental capacities! Here was an opening to new powers and purposes. I felt pity for Milesian. Let him hang back. If he feared these majestic forces, I did not. With them I would settle the vain and intricate disputations that plagued these troubled times.

I was charged with the most lucid thoughts and schemes. I corrected doctrinal errors in a brilliant debate with the Holy Father. I planned a university—nay seven universities! I designed new and amazing machines that could fly, and collect the powers of the sun, and irresistible engines of war to bring peace to the intrigue-filled West. . . .

But this is only the crudest rendering of my mentations as I stood before the Dragonskull. I felt an irresistible urge to lay my hands upon its forehead of polished bone. Trembling, I gave a darting glance to Milesian, ere he ambush my desire. He stood impassive, hands gently folded. Yet at that moment, I heard Eugnostos's couplet. *Find the*

thinker not the thought. . . . What did he mean? To turn my attention from the thoughts to their source? To test its truth, I need only quell for a moment the engagements of my mind; it would be a simple act of will. I tried but quickly found myself wandering down another corridor of speculations. Again and again I tried, and each time was soon caught up in some new mental diversion.

Then, amidst the glittering insights, came the notion that perhaps the rush of thoughts that so enraptured me *were not mine,* but a *natural event,* like a river. And thus my soul separated gently from that torrent and observed it, with unutterable stillness. I became a witness, empty and light. All those glorious cogitations were revealed as a chimera, as wheels of flame that spun in the darkness but illumined it not. And even as I watched them, they fell still.

Thus I awoke from the Dragon spell. My hands were clenched, my body damp with sweat. Involuntarily I stepped back from the gleaming bone. Where I had just embraced its power, intoxicated, now the same force streamed right through me, as sunlight through the most transparent Venetian glass. "We may go now," said Milesian.

He backed out of the cave, and I followed, till we stood on the threshold. Peering into the shadows I now saw two empty sockets in the jaws where the great incisor teeth had been. And for an instant I perceived, as if by subtle sight, the finest tangle of mystic crimson threads emanating in all directions from those awful pits.

I stood rooted to the spot. "Come, friend," he said again, "let us now leave this grim place."

My spirit was in a remarkable state of quiescence. Milesian motioned me to a path that soon plunged down a rocky incline. The stones were slippery, my footing failed, and I found myself careening wildly down a darkened defile. Gaining the bottom I saw that I had returned to the isle and the path along the sea. Milesian moved silently beside me and took my arm. "Let us take some dinner. And (here he smiled for the first time) *per amore Unicornis,* do watch your step—the tide is rising."

And so he led me back to his home and hearth, where Ibn awaited. Before long a servant brought us a great round oatcake and a bowl of curds, and we shared it in silence, and of that I was glad.

We were put up on some clean straw pallets in a small cell next to his room, and I slept far past my accustomed hour. Ibn was gone, no doubt off exploring. I rose and stood for some time at the window. The sun was already high in the sky, and streamed in the opening, which faced the south. I must have remained there for some time, bathed in a tranquil state, gazing out into the bay which cupped the mount. All traces of yesterday's mist were gone and the blue swells ran beneath a firm breeze, sparkling as if cast with jewels. From this lofty perch my sight flew out straight to the horizon and the deep Atlantic waters and I recalled the adventure of the evening past, but it was already distant, like a half-forgotten tale.

Milesian greeted me simply, asking only if I wished some porridge, then ladled my oats into a trencher and asked if we ate such horse food as this in Italy—acting, it seemed, as if nothing of any import had occurred the eve before.

"Sir," I cried, "am I mad? Or yestereve did we not enter the Timeless Land and there see wondrous things? Who are you, that moves so easily between the worlds?"

He laid down his pot. "Well said, Magnalucius. In the name of the true Celi Dé I greet and honor you. You met the Dragonskull and passed its test."

"Milesian," I said, "I seek the Tooth."

"I know," he said. "but let us sup, and talk more later, for our meal grows cold."

That afternoon Ibn returned and busied himself repairing our boots by the window, while Milesian and I sat at his oaken board and he continued my education. "Magh Dá Cheo. At last night's gloaming, you and I did venture there. Elsewhere it is called Brocileande, and Sidh, and Nim, and Caer Sidd Drago. *In its rivers Salmon speaking, Unicorn in forests dreaming, Dragon deep in caverns brooding.* It is vast, but narrow are the gates that lead therein, for the Laws that protect the Realm are ordered and clear. Chú stole the teeth and forced them back, to here, his earthly seat. The Law was broken. Years rolled on, his line failed, and the isle was left to gulls and fisherfolk until we Celi Dé came and took guardianship. In time others arrived and forced their claims upon the rock. But we have not broken trust. Always we have kept a Guardian here. *We wait, we watch, we guard the gate to Magh Dá Cheo.* Yet now the Perilous Tooth is gone."

"The Tooth was here?" I cried.

The title page of Fondla's last journal.

"Did you not know? Ah, but I did not either, not until made Guardian. Before me was the saintly Dyvdd, before him, Fondla." Milesian composed himself. "We Reclaimers work in solitude, so it was not strange that when Dyvdd came to relieve Fondla, that monk had not been heard from for more than a decade. Alas, when Dyvdd land-ed he found Fondla lost, the Tooth stolen, this room in ruin. In sorrow Dyvdd took up the guardianship."

"Had you met Fondla, Milesian?"

"No. Dyvdd had, for he had visited him many years before. It was to him that Fondla revealed he had found the Dragontooth and brought it with him to the Isle."

"Fondla had *found* the thing?"

"Yes—if *found* is the right word. He told Dyvdd he had been *the hand of God* in the matter. Who can say, perhaps he was. He never revealed from where he got the thing. Perhaps it was a former owner who came in force to reclaim the Tooth."

"Do we know when that would have been?" said I.

Milesian shrugged. "Any time in Fondla's years of silence. Perhaps Brother Dyvdd knew, but alas he passed away unexpectedly and left no accounts."

"Then you were appointed Guardian?"

"Yes. The year after King Charles died. By the time I came here, all witnesses to the crime were long dispersed. Those were dangerous times for all."

"So, another mystery," said I. "Let us find the beginning. When did Fondla come to the Isle?"

"That is recorded as forty-six years ago."

"Good. And if we know not when Fondla met his end, do we know when Dyvdd discovered the crime?"

Milesian counted on his fingers, "Thirteen years later." He shook his big head slow-ly. "Ah Fondla! Would that I had known him! He was a brilliant man, and his mind dwelt on a lofty platform. Look—" He stepped to the masonry wall and gently slid out a block and set it upon the ground. "I found this spot the second year of my stay. These are Fondla's journals, year by year. He started keeping them three years before his end. But mark, not one date in them! The man did not sully his thoughts with the tracks of mundane time. Look at these entries: no mention of events whatsoever, a diary of the spirit only.

Here: his last year, his last entry, written, one imagines, the day he perished and the Tooth was taken: 'Light and hope do ever remain beyond the doleful storm, as whole and sacred the circle escapes the Quadrature of the Lune.'"

"*What?* May I see?" I asked.

The page was filled with geometrical drawings; others had similiar esoteric entries. He had designed a title page for the yearbook in the manner of an old Irish gospel. The work was fine, if unfinished. I stared at it as if it would render up an answer to the riddle.

"Mark the details," said Ibn, who had silently come over. "Though the work has its beauty, it is full of minor errors. A sign of haste perhaps?"

"—Or lack of craft," said Milesian. "You have a decent eye, Moor, but I do not believe Fondla was actually trained in illumination." He tugged gently at the page, and it came loose without resistance. "Keep this, Magnalucius. Perhaps there is something you may learn from it, or keep it as a good luck token, a saintly relic, a gift of the Celi Dé. Find the Tooth."

"I thank you," said I. "It is a thing of beauty. Perhaps it will reveal something of the Tooth's career. But you can guess nothing of the Tooth before or after Fondla? Who else might have known of the thing?" We paused in thought. "Christ's beard!" I cried. "Where was I born?" I went to my bag and found the printed woodcut that Nural Din had given me. "Here is a picture of the very thing."

Milesian let out a hiss of breath. "So this is Fondla's Tooth."

"And by the evidence of this page we know it has appeared since its taking, or immediately before."

"How so?" asked the monk.

"Because it is a printed page, and such skills have been in use but fifty years," said Ibn, catching the drift of my thought.

"May I see?" said Milesian. I handed him the sheet and he scanned both sides carefully. "Aha, what is this on the lower corner? Could it be a symbol put by the printer? It has an English crown. If you could find this printer, he ought to remember his customer."

91

"How many printers can there be in England?" I said. "We shall find this shop. I have a cousin who commerces in English wool and keeps an English home. He could assist me in this search."

Our boatman need not wait another day. Tomorrow morning we will sail.

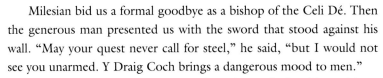 Milesian bid us a formal goodbye as a bishop of the Celi Dé. Then the generous man presented us with the sword that stood against his wall. "May your quest never call for steel," he said, "but I would not see you unarmed. Y Draig Coch brings a dangerous mood to men."

I have never learned swordplay, but Ibn took the thing with an easy familiarity. Then the sail was up and full, and our captain expertly guided the prow towards a distant printer's shop. Onward!

June the 17th

The port was clogged with merchant vessels and bedeviled with shouting kingsmen. As best we could tell, they were searching all departing ships for a highborn spy. Little attention was paid to an itinerant gnostic and his Moorish servant arriving in a small boat with the fate of the age in their hands. We made our way without incident to a smelly quayside inn. On first assay, these English are vigorous, arrogant, and suspicious of all foreigners. Indeed they seem not to trust each other. To my surprise, Ibn displayed an excellent facility with their language. I fear if I am to make my way about alone I must learn the tongue as well, coarse as it is.

June the 18th

If this town is no worse than any other, it certainly is no better. The lame and infirm are abused, the malefactor rides in silk. Men bicker over the color of flowers, and leave their daughters to whoredom. Everything has its price, including, if tavern gossip runs true, the kingdom itself. Nevertheless, these people are industrious, with such wealth that silver

STATION IX
The City

candlesticks are found in every inn. We have taken new rooms in a more respectable place on Fetter Lane (some goldsmithing guilds display their wares nearby). Now to find cousin Anselmo. Also: I have been pondering the parchmenter's words. If indeed Severinus had traded the *Poetics* for the Periadam, then there might be a record of the transaction—even the stone's origins—in the Curia. From this, might we not discern something of the path of the Tooth? I must contrive to write my old ally Giacomo in Rome. If any one could ferret this information out of the Curia it would be he. I sent Ibn to find the Anselmo Fortuna house.

June the 19th

Anselmo lives on a certain Carters Street or Lane. We arrived unheralded at noon, and though we had not met since childhood he embraced me warmly, and offered me all his resources. I could not have asked for more. A coasting vessel in his service departs Saturday for Rome and will carry my letter to the Papal offices. Further, Anselmo will arrange to transport Giacomo's reply, and I should have my answer in six weeks or less! I will use the time to study the language. Here again the good Anselmo comes to my aid, and will send a tutor to my lodgings tomorrow. Finally, he knows a bookseller who he is sure will identify my broadsheet. The grand pattern holds.

June the 20th

Robert Wynd arrived smartly at five. He is a smallish fellow, intelligent and eager to please, a university student who tutors to supplement his income. We spoke in Latin briefly, then he insisted that all intercourse between us be conducted in English. An unorthodox method, but I am progressing rapidly, for I have a gift for languages.

July the 9th

We have the trail! First I found Anselmo's hunchbacked old bookseller, who straight off identified the woodcut as the work of a certain Grimston Bros. in St. Brides. It was not far. Grimston Bros. occupied a large well-timbered building with a signboard practically the duplicate of my imprint. Inside their office a portly manager with blackened fingertips squinted when I showed him the page, and said he did not know it. When I pointed out the mark, he scowled. "We must have done it all right, but before my time, when the place was run by Uncle Marlow."

"And where might I find the man?" I asked. "Under six feet of St. Mary's sod," said he. But as he turned to other business, a wiry little codger in a greasy leather apron came bustling from the workshop behind, wiping lampblack from his hands.

"The screw's gone loose again," he began. Then his eyes fell on the page I held. "Oh-ho," he said, "remember that job? The Witch-King's alchemist said we—"

"Nat!" cut in his master, giving him a look fierce enough to raise old Marlow from his resting-place. "Aren't you better be stirring your pulp? Hop now."

Nat knew his duty, and shot back into the working rooms. Not a word more could I get from my ill-mannered proprietor, but I did not press the issue. I did not know the full tale yet, but it did not take a philosopher to perceive that when a Witch-King's alchemist is your customer, a little fear and secrecy may be involved, even at a generation's remove. But I had glimpsed my quarry. *The Witch-King's alchemist!*

More. Returned to our rooms with this tale. Ibn asked to see the page and now he scrutinized it carefully. "But here!" he cried. "Look at this." I came to his side, and he showed me a sign hidden in its design. "What is it, a glyph of alchemy?"

It seems to be. But what it means and how it figures in this quest I do not know.

July the 15th

A dubious event has left me sorely disturbed. Our days have been marked by the most melodic pealing of the hours, and this morning I set out to find the church of such beautiful bells. I had not gone a block before I saw I had forgotten my staff. (I know this city well enough now to keep oak by my side.) Returning to the inn, I found one of the servants cleaning my room. Or so I took him to be, for he had on an apron and linen on his arm. He was standing by the table where I had laid my journals, and quickly excused himself when I entered. There was something familiar about his face, but it was fully a minute before it came. The curious fellow in the inn! *Johann Faust.* I bolted in pursuit of the incubus, but he had vanished. I put the journals in my leather packet-sack, slung it on my shoulder, and set out again. Henceforth they will not leave my side. *Di omni pecatore guarda nos*!

St. Swithans: Sweet bells, yard filled with gossiping monks.

Good fortune. Last night after lessons I put the riddle of the Witch-King to Robert Wynd. He had no answer, but said he personally knew the apothecary, Master Abaris. If I would accompany him tomorrow, we might put the question to him.

We found Abaris behind a counter in his shop, bent over his mortar and grinding an amber substance with extraordinary zeal. I was struck by his concentration. He was thin, no older than thirty-five, and wore a plain blue doublet. A loose velvet cap covered his long dark hair.

"Master Abaris?" said Wynd nervously after a moment.

"Robert Wynd!" he replied without looking up or breaking stroke. "Be brief. If I fail this compounding I shall be displeased."

"Sir, do you know who might be the Witch-King's alchemist?"

"Meddling again, Bob?" he said, without looking up. "The Witch-King's alchemist? That would be—what did we call him? Aha, yes *Demon John*. Or was it John the Demon?" He laughed. "A dabbler, a nobody who affected that he lived at the seat of Arthur. He was hardly a—one moment—*done*!" He gave a final stroke with his pestle, looked up and saw me standing behind Wynd. His manner changed abruptly. His pale gray eyes took my measure.

"Pardon, sir, I did not know I had company. Wynd! You blow this way and that, and forget to properly present your friends."

"Master Abaris," said the flustered tutor, "may I present Master Magnalucius from Florence, a most learned sage following a noble quest through England."

This introduction took me aback. In our daily lessons, Wynd had gathered bits and pieces of my undertaking, but I had warned him that I wished to travel in the shadow of anonymity. "Master Magnalucius," the fool continued enthusiastically, "is of the illuminati just as yourself."

I must have winced, for Abaris himself rescued the situation with admirable delicacy. "As are you, dear Robert, for all good men bear the light of illumination."

I appreciated Abaris's tact, but, as the peasants say, *If the pigs get out, even the Pope can't wish them back.* The conversation circled with pleasantries at first, but drew quickly to the esoteric, and I perceived how learned was this fellow Abaris on every subject that arose. Was he part of the pattern? Could I safely enlist him in the Quest?

Wynd had a tutorial, and so excused himself. I turned the conversation to the subject of talismans. What truths, I wondered, might the legends of the Grail, or the unicorn's horn, or the Dragontooth conceal?

"A slippery area," he said with a disarming smile. "One can prove a thing exists, never that it does not." Then, as in confidence, "The Tooth, as you must know, is nothing other than the *materium profundum*, the *Azoth* of the Templars. And you have probably discovered its connection with the Thirty-Six Invisibles, who live outside of time?" He lowered his voice. "Of course, Magnalucius, we are aware of your search."

"We?" said I to hide my confusion. "You refer to an order?"

"To be sure. One that has existed through all time—and by many names," said he. "But time, as the common man lives it, is an illusion to which you and I will not fall prey. The Dragontooth, of course, hangs outside *before* and *after*. Is it not the gilded pinion of the Sepheroth that links history with eternity?" His eyes brightened as he warmed to the subject. Now the Tooth was one of the *elemental virtues*, next *a compound of the coiled serpent fire.*

I was dazzled by the poetry of his thought—but what was this man, so eloquent in dragonlore, saying? Was the tooth real—or only a mystic symbol? I felt on the verge of grasping the secret key to the whole adventure, but I needed to insert something tangible into our discourse. Reaching into my bag I found Nural Din's woodcut. "And what of such as this?" I asked.

He gave it only a glance. "Yes, yes." said he, "regard the fabled Tooth. Perhaps a forgery, perhaps not. Does it matter? Is not this whole world a forgery of the Real?" He handed it back to me. "Men wish to believe in talismans filled with arcane powers. Do they exist?

Only because we have convinced ourselves of it. But should the true scientist not pursue the *dragonis aeternum*, the alchemical dragon of *eternity*? But yes! In this very city there are those steeped in this knowledge." He went to the outer door and barred it. "Look!" He reached behind a curtain and fetched a thick portfolio stuffed with loose manuscripts and papers. "I should not reveal this, but I perceive you are indeed one of the illuminati. Here is the new canon of the age, the *Tractate Dragonis Splendorium*. It is not a book, but a living thing, growing as the wisdom of our order grows."

I reached to examine it, but he touched my wrist. "Not yet. The initiate must first submit his own investigations to the Archon, that he may be found serious. Then all doors are opened."

It was late and I excused myself, saying that I would consider his words. I left discomfited. Have I gone old and rigid? I am well aware how the dullard's mind recoils from the new. I do not know why, but I made my way then to Saint Sulpice and sat in the shadows while monks chanted Vespers.

August the 8th

I must decide on our path. A morning of walking and thinking. Some conclusions: *Primero*: I do not yet have a clue where the Tooth lies. *Segundo*: Abaris's fey treatment of "John the Demon" tells me to set that course aside for now. *Tercero*: There is something unsettling about Abaris, but perhaps it is only the subtle nature of his thought. There is probably some risk in leaguing with him, but much to gain. If he and his Archons, or whatever they call themselves, think the Dragontooth is only a symbol, let them! Those Tractates may indeed bring this quest to a swift conclusion. Yet I cannot quite convince myself to throw in with him.

At noon a messenger arrived from Anselmo carrying a letter for me with the papal mark!

The Vatican
My dear Magnalucius,

May the sacred blood bring blessing to your life.

With what pleasure, my most esteemed Magnalucius, we have received your missive. Your work shall always command our interest. As regarding the information that you requested we must tell you obtaining it was very difficult and in truth almost cost us our reputation. The tale we now convey lay under the seals of the Papal Indefata and had to be procured by measures I hope never to repeat. I trust the matter is of considerable importance.

On 23 November year last, Cardinal Barnaba, chief financial conciliator of the papal bank authorized the exchange of one "curious glasslike ball" in the papal collection for two books in the property of the monastery in question. Said books were an edition of Aristotle's Poetics, and an infamous volume of lecherous tales whose title I shall not commit to paper. De gustibus non disputatum est.

I undertook to learn more of the nature of this "curious glasslike ball." On 3 April 1471, the Ball was conveyed by an envoy from the Archbishop of Canterbury directly to His Holiness Alexander VI. The only surviving identification from that time is a brief note on the papal calendar that the said diadem had been found in "the Holy Isle" the year before, and had been judged worthless, but of possible historical interest. His Holiness then assigned it to the papal reliquaries.

There, six years later it was handled by a filing clerk, a young priest, who reported faintness, dizzy spells and a certain "radiance of vision" as a result. These symptoms persisted for some time despite treatment by the papal physicians. The Ball was held accountable and an Imprimatur Daemonicus placed upon it. It was then placed in a vault where it remained until the aforementioned transaction.

The scarcity of documentation might lead one to speculate that there may have been some high official action associated with the Ball later deemed improper, and the record expunged. That is all we know.

Also as you asked, a letter was sent to Abbot Longinus regrettably asserting that the Scriptorium Oscura of the Curia could not possibly release you into his services.

If it is within our power to be of further use, command.

Giacomo Fantuzzi, Bds., Int.

August the 9th

 A new light on our affairs! Took Giacomo's letter post haste to an amateur historian whom I met at St. Swithans yard last week, one Henry Derville. He knew at once the "sacred isle" of the Ball. More: he promptly identified the Witch-King as well.

20

Conferred with Ibn. He is keen for the sacred isle. "There would be a fine odor of sanctity wherever the Hesed was," said he. And the Tooth may be nearby as well. Yes, I am convinced. Here is the direction to pursue. If fruitless, we will return and pick up with the Archon. I will send the kitchen-boy with a note to Abaris thanking him for his offer, but that we must be off on our search by the morrow. Pilgrims again! I hope he will understand.

August the 10th

Anselmo insisted on sending us off with a proper feast, and we had to accept. Returning to the inn much later than our custom, we had just turned onto Fetter when three questionable-looking men sidling up the street toward us filled me with foreboding. They were armed and passing a bottle. Suddenly a door burst open next to us and four soldiers tumbled out, laughing. The other men slipped into the darkness of an alley. I glanced at Ibn, and we fell in behind the soldiers up Dyers St. We continued thus for a half-dozen blocks, then Ibn nudged me and turned into the shadows of the guildhall. I followed. Silent as mice we waited. There was no sign of the cutpurses. The steps of the soldiers grew fainter and died. The only sound was the thin wail of a baby in a far-off tenement. Ibn knew the streets better than I and led us back in a circuitous route to the lower end of Fetters. As we approached the butcher shop, we both heard the faintest snick of steel from within the shadows of its entrance. A clammy sweat spread across my forehead. "Run!" Ibn whispered, and he bolted ahead like a deer. My legs would not move. A figure leapt out of the shadows at the Moor. Starlight glimmered on a long knife.

Filled with a sudden strength, I let out a bellow that split the night. "Ibn! To me! To me!"

In an instant the scene was transformed. Ibn sprang to one side, and the other two outlaws leapt out at me. One tripped, cursing, and took the other down as well. Ibn's pursuer spun around to see what had befallen his companions, and Ibn fetched him a tremendous wallop, knocking him to the ground, then ran back to my side. A dozen curs set up a racket, windows were flung open overhead, and the contents of a chamber pot arched out of an upper window onto the rogues. They scrambled off in different directions, and the street was suddenly ours again. The barking spread in widening circles and slowly died. I felt suddenly light-headed. Imperturbable as ever, Ibn flashed me a grin I could see even in starlight. "Quite the dragon's roar you have, my lord," he said, and guided us up the street to our quarters.

Who were the cutpurses? Ordinary thieves or hired assassins? No matter, we still have our lives—*and the journals.* Tomorrow we wagon west, and then take ship. But I fear our dangers are not over.

August the 13th

Second day on the road, our wain broke an axletree on a pothole. The coachman blamed the groom, the groom blamed the king, and I learned some truly poetic maledictions. Luckily a nearby hamlet was building a church to the good St. Nichole and had several smithy fires burning. Ibn, myself, and our fellow passenger, a dour doctor of humanities, made our way to a large mill which served as a public house.

With time to waste I set out to explore our surroundings. The Town Mill was set where the high road crossed the river Kennet. The area around was wooded, and I found a pleasant path that followed the river bank. Great blue dragonflies darted over the surface of the water, and handsome trout glided among the waterweeds. After a mile I came upon a well-laden wagon encamped by the bank. A tall fellow in leather breeches hunted the shallows for crayfish. A large lady and three brats lay napping under a tree, and a smallish woman sat on a fallen log by the shore gazing into the water. By the picturesque way they wore their clothing I took them for gypsy folk.

STATION X
The Gypsy

The driver looked up, assessed me as harmless, grunted *Hola*, and went back to his job. The woman on the log pulled an embroidered shawl over her head. She was not young, but strongly built, with the dark look of the Celts. I am sure she painted her lips, for as she turned her look to me, I saw they were unnaturally red. I returned her gaze.

"What is it that you want?" she said finally.

"Nothing. I am a traveler; my coach is at the mill."

"No, no," she said, making a motion with her hand as if brushing my answer away, "Not that. There is something you are wanting."

"I am called Magnalucius, and I am a pilgrim new to this country."

"Where are you from? Come here, come here," she motioned to me, and I obeyed. "I am from Italy."

She began plucking long pieces of grass. "You are a churchman?"

I laughed, "No dame, I am not."

"A scholar?"

"Once."

"Have you ever seen a witch burnt?"

"Thanks be to God," said I, "I have not, for that is an abomination."

"Do you know the Goddess?"

"I honor her as the Virgin."

She rose and took my wrist and sat me down on the log so that we faced each other. "This is a gift," she said, and moved closer, so that her knees pressed on either side of mine. I flushed. *This is not wise*, I thought, but the fellow in the stream took no notice of us. She took my right hand in both of hers.

"You are earth and air," she said.

Her fingers were very warm and moved around my hand with a firm and probing touch, as if she were seeing with her hands and not her eyes. She traced the lines in my palms.

"What do you carry? What is it? There is something bright over your heart. What are you seeking?" I felt she was drawing me into her. My mind muddled.

Her legs relaxed. "You are beyond me," she said. "You must see Y Derwydd." She fumbled with some trinkets on her sash and untied something.

"I, Doona, am giving you this," she said, and pressed into my hand a small bronze ring.

"Why?"

"Because it came from the well of Mother Uma." She pressed it into my hand. "Now you must give me something."

"What do you wish?"

"Anything."

"Anything?" I reached into my packet bag and found her a half piece of rough drawing paper.

She approved. "Make your mark upon it!"

I took a stick of ocher and drew the seal of the Collegium.

"A sign!" she said, and folding the paper carefully, tucked it into her bodice. What witch-magic was this woman doing? Seeing my questioning look, she said, "Do you not do *Kris subhuuth*?" She searched for a word. "—*Connecting*?"

"Connecting?"

"*Doona!*" There was a call from the drover, who was starting a fire. She spoke quickly.

"*Yes, my lord*! High fortune runs round you, do you know? So many *subhuut lines*! So I wish to take something of yours and keep it at my well where Uma lives. But not like a thief. There must be a giving to you of something that came from there. Then the lines connect strong and balanced." She hurried off.

I returned to the mill and told Ibn the story. "*Subhanallah*!" he exclaimed softly. "I should have thought of that. The sorcerers of the Persians say that an ill fate befalls one who takes an enchanted thing unless they leave something in its place to satisfy the *jinns*. Let us look again at the snake!" He left and returned shortly with the copper serpent, but we could read no more in it than before.

Our professor sat on some sacks at a window with his nose in a book. "Sir," said I to him, "have you a knowledge of antiquity?"

"In some measure," he said. "I teach the Trivium, but I entertain an interest in peerage, and am regarded as somewhat versed in the histories."

"Then we are blessed," said I. "Could I persuade you to look at this odd discovery? I am curious of its origin."

Ibn brought him the copper serpent. He wrinkled his nose. "The work of pagan Britons," he said, "but it bears no distinguishing characteristics." He turned it over. "What is this? Observe, here we have an interesting addition. They used a coin to make its eye."

"Do you recognize it?"

"Of course. It is an Alfred-pence, quite old."

"And can you say where it came from? What place?" said I.

"Came from? What do you mean? You are the ones who found it."

"Perhaps, my Lord, where the coin was made?" offered Ibn.

"Ah, you must learn to say what you mean. It was made in ———. A mint worked there in Saxon times, when it was an outpost against the Danes."

I thanked him profusely. We would have to change our itinerary. Could the end of the Quest be at hand? Onward!

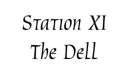

Station XI
The Dell

August the 17th

Should have studied English geography more thoroughly. We have come not to a wild outpost where a dragontooth would properly be hid, but a comfortable town. Took rooms in the Blue Boar. What now?

August the 19th

I have poked and pried about town, but all I have discovered is that no one here is without a learned opinion. And for what am I looking? A Druid priest? Abaris's coiled serpent fire? A sign in the sky? This is mad. Indeed, I might proceed better if I were mad. Then at least, I could wander about with a lantern singing doggerel about lost dragonteeth. In the end it is only speculation that the Tooth is hereabouts at all. Better we pursue our original path.

I chanced this morning to hear Ibn singing softly to himself. It was a song of vast and empty deserts and caravans and solitude. I thought, *I am a son of another land and there is a different music in me, of olive groves and summer rains.* This gulf shall always endure between our souls. But such yearning in his song! Later he went for new provisions. Having abandoned the search I wandered outside the town through freshly scythed hayfields. I came to the confluence of two broad streams, a mess of hazel and furze, bog myrtle, and wild gooseberries. A wooded spot attracted my attention and, entering, I found a dell. Mayflies shimmered in the warm sunlight. It seemed that I knew this place. The twisted yew, the tumbled boulders. . . The feeling was so pervasive I took out my journal to speculate upon its cause. Going through its pages, my eye was arrested by an idle sketch of an imaginary woody scene done months ago. I almost dropped my pen: I had sketched the very dell wherein I sat!

What was this enchantment? The Unicorn! Somehow I knew this was his design. But how? Then I remembered—had I not learned long ago that in our dreams the Unicorn may come and show us things? But I had never concerned myself with this blessing, because I am a sound sleeper and rarely dream. *Wait,* I thought, *perhaps I do dream, but in waking forget?* That being the case, might not the images of such rare dreams show themselves in other ways? Perhaps in my idle and imaginary scratchings they could emerge? Why not? Whether by Unicorn or sweet chance sent, I found myself upon a spot where destiny was ripe. I'd sit and wait. I had the day.

On warm summer days time can stand still. My vision grew acute. Across the clearing I observed with perfect clarity a spider's web; each thread stood out sharp and separate. I saw the tiny meandering lines on the bark of a fallen beech. I saw in the shadows beneath it— what?—*a slinking worm!* Or was it only the way the shadows lay? I could not tell, but I felt no fear. It was as if the world had grown transparent, and I looked through it into the Other World, and there it was dark of night.

Thus the vision came. It was night; the moon was full and un-cannily bright. The boulders stood upright, higher than a man, and behind them the encircling trees towered thick and old. A man in ancient dress came into the clearing, followed by a great wolf-dog. By the One! I saw that the man was the same I had encountered in my troubled dream at my brother's house. He stood before the rocks and spoke. They groaned, and moved apart as if alive. Then the old man opened a pouch that hung at his waist and lifted out the Dragontooth. It was greater than I had thought. He held it by the handle and spoke to it, as if it were a living thing. Then he put it in the tomb and closed the stones and left, the wolf-dog beside him.

A veil descended. Though I was in the same place, I knew I was in another time. Men with torches came now, led by a little boy who ran up to the stones, now all overgrown. He got on his belly and wriggled through a crack inside and came back out, and the men fell upon the stones with iron bars and levers and toppled one. Two who were leaders stepped forward and began to argue. One was dressed in a long gray gown, the other wore boots and armor and a battle cloak of white. Each entered and came out, solemnly carrying a Dragontooth. Then a bright light shone in my eyes, bright as the light of day, and my head throbbed, and I lay senseless upon the ground.

The Tooth had come here and had gone. That was the vision. I knew it was true. Ibn and I would continue on our appointed path. Someday I would know what all these glimpses meant. Until then I would content myself like the blind man examining the elephant, knowing one part at a time. Tomorrow we pick up our old trail to the Cave. Onward!

[*Previous page missing*]

. . . over a small rise, and the blue waters spread before us. "Now, see!" Ellen laughed, "I have brought you to sight of the shore and out yonder lies the Isle. Holiness lies in every rock and rill. A plague upon the foreign hand that lays to waste a place such as that! We shall not forget. Are you come to fast and pray?"

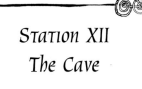

Station XII
The Cave

I had not thought of that. But as quickly as she asked, I told her yes.

"That I knew the first I saw you, sir. Yonder on the rocky strand are fisherfolk who take pilgrims over the water. Now good sir and heathen too, if you would reward me I have my own fortunes to attend."

In somnio me currere detrebant et eram sicut peregrinus in urbe incognita, qua turres altae et populi circumdantes viderentur. Me autem nemo vidit. Gradiebar miro modo, nunc caput ad caelum extendens nunc serpens super terram humilis. Omnis domus et omnis aula me magistrum agnoscebat, et nulla porta et nullum secretum non mihi obviam erat.

Fortitudo mea sicut adamantina voluntas mea sicut terram, et horrore et exultatione certus laetus eram quia ego flactus sum drago ille quam superbus galea bam. Repebam, serpbam, me conciebam hic et illic, sinuosam tergum meum in cyclis subtexis et divi tteus.

We paid this woman her fee, and more besides, for I am sure we owed our skins to her, and she strode off, as valiant a soul as ever I have known. Ibn and I led our horses down the shore to where a handful of rough-built boats were drawn up alongside their owners' huts. A few filthy children peeped out from a noisome doorway. An old scoundrel mending nets acknowledged us with a grunt.

"Greetings, fisherman," said I. "You give passage to the Holy Isle?"

The man looked us up and down with squinty eyes.

"Foreigners?"

"I am a Christian on pilgrimage."

"And the infidel?"

"My servant. He stays behind."

He spat on the pebbles, and tied another knot in his net. "As well. A black and unbaptized infidel will not set foot in any boat of mine."

So saying he went back to his nets as if we no longer existed.

I palavered with the man, and we struck a price to take me over and three days hence to fetch me back. I took no worry for Ibn, for if ever there was a fellow happier in his own company I have not met him. I handed him my pack, and feeling a sudden coursing of affection for the man, embraced him. "*Pace vobiscum,*" he said softly in my ear. "*Mysterium tremendum in te occultatum.*"

Then into the man's flimsy bark. He tended the sail, I bailed, and prayed no great wind would rise.

"You know the cave?" I asked. He nodded and changed course slightly. We finally scraped bottom, and pointing to a path, he swung about and was off without a nod.

I climbed the path and found the opening. I knew at once there was no Tooth inside; the place was too benign. Still, it was a place of revelation, and if not a Tooth then guidance might be found. I climbed into the rocky hole and found my place, and waited. Evening came. A string of geese flew past, the sky turned green and gold, and slowly faded into night.

I ached. Shadows pressed all around, and in truth most of that watch I rued the undertaking. Yet toward morning a warm wind came up and drove away the damp, and if no revelation had come to me, neither had any evil. The second night brought a measure of peace. Perhaps the peace of Jesus, for it was simple and forgiving. I resolved to find my vision on the third and final night. I laid myself open, as best I knew how. But instead of vision, the grace of silence came. I will not complain. When the gods wish to speak to a man, they do it how and when they will. I left the cave at first light, and laid myself down in the grass above the strand, and fell asleep, and dreamed.

In the dream I was restless and roamed around an unknown high-towered city that was filled with a press of people. But none saw me. I was moving in the strangest manner: I could raise myself to twice my natural height, or as I wished, move low to the earth. I was master of every house and hall, and no door and no secret could be shut to me, for my strength was adamant, my will was iron. I knew with a secret thrill that *I was become the dragon*. How I reveled in my nature! I glided, I glanced dartingly about, powerfully coiling and uncoiling my gleaming length.

How can I describe that state? The lives of men were as chaff in the wind, and years were as days. I wish I could say that I was not myself, but it is not so. I was myself, or some portion thereof: keen and powerful and superior. I went into a stone tower, and climbed to its roof. Spread out before me were all the places of the world. Everything was buttressed and wrapped with iron, and I was pleased. Then I descended to the second story, which was a treasury, and coiled myself in a brazen casket there, and spread my thoughts around the world.

The boatman's hoot pierced the dream and pulled me out so swiftly that I remembered it, complete. It is the vision that I sought. But it has left me troubled, for it is a portent that I can not interpret.

Brak (as so the old man called himself) had pulled his boat up on the shingle. I climbed in and we shoved off. He must have spent his fare on brew, for he tacked back sullenly muttering to himself. After a while (and for no apparent reason), his thoughts emerged into coherent speech.

"He was the great one, he was. It was the true faith then. Now *we* catch the fish, *we* fill their plates . . ." He lapsed into mumbling again. Then: "Fasted and found it he did. Still and all, he should never have thrown it away, but who is Brakman to be telling a saint his business?

109

Well I could have told him magic things never stay lost. If he'd 'a' left it with us, we'd still have it now. Then things would have been set aright."

"Found what?" I asked in a flat voice, trying (if it were possible) to be just another thought in this simple man's mind. It worked, for he replied in the same muttering way, "The Tooth, what else? The holy Tooth. Was ours by rights, us who's borned and dies right here."

Was the man grumbling about ills suffered centuries past, as simple folk sometimes do? "But it wouldn't stay lost," I said.

"No, not that thing. Drug up by Clonta boys in their net, and given to the king. The fools. Fagh! Now it's gone, and we fisherfolk still gnaw on bones."

"And all this was by your granda's time?" said I.

"Granda's time? He'd heard the tale from his granda, and he from his, and . . ." The fellow suddenly narrowed his eyes, as if he had just realized I was in the boat. "Hey now, what are you asking?"

"When did they find the Tooth?"

"Tooth? Who knows nothing about a tooth! And if you're a Christian as you claim, you'll know even less. Now let me sail my boat." There was no more from the man, only mumblings, but I had heard what the gods had wanted. And I had found my vision. Where to now? To find Demon John. An arduous trip, and I weary of the road. But, Onward.

September the 25th

Every innkeeper hereabouts has heard of John. He lived here, moved there, was abroad, or dead and buried. Shifting fortunes had turned this king's favorite into an outcast. Finally, I was led to a white-washed cottage in the hills a half-day's ride southwest of town. It was rough country, where wolves

Station XIII
The Witch-King's Alchemist

and wild men roam in winter. The wall surrounding the little place was half run to ruin, but the yard was neatly kept.

Around the side of the cottage, we saw a woman kneeling and planting flowers. I guessed she was forty, but still pink-cheeked. Round her waist was tied the colored sash of a gypsy Celt.

110

"Hola!" I called out, but she only looked dumbly at us. Ibn and I dismounted, but approaching her, I saw that she was planting a fresh-dug grave.

"Lady," I said, "we have traveled here from far-off lands, but we have come on a sad day, I see."

Then tears welled up in her eyes and she cried, "You're late, you're late, whoever you are, he'll never speak no more." She started wiping her hands, and moaning, and rocking back and forth. Having seen these people thus lose themselves to endless keening, I pulled the Periadam from my neck and knelt beside her with it cradled in my hand. "My lady," I said, "by the gods and the saints and the Creator of all, *what is this*?"

She stared, dazed. Then recognition bloomed in her eyes and she ceased her rocking. "Why, it's the dew of the Unicorn, that Johnny did seek," she said in a wavering voice, and laid a timid finger upon it.

"I heard the curlews in the heather," she whispered after a minute, and removed her hand, and wept. "For twenty years he sought this sweet holy thing," she sobbed, "and today it comes to me."

She wiped her eyes. "And so I'd better be counting my blessings then, wouldn't you say, and not go a-wailing any more." And she composed herself and led us into her small home. It was comfortably filled with a curious variety of appointments. Turkish rugs were spread on the oiled earthen floor, the furniture was sound, the mantle was set with good pewter plates. I noticed philter and crucible—alchemist's gear—upon a shelf.

This woman was a simple soul, and having thus given us her trust, she felt no hesitation in unburdening her story.

"Johnny was an artist, you know. Not a painter, though he could draw tolerably well if he wished, but an artist in his soul, if you know what I mean. Such a man! A traveler, a swordsman, he did alchemy too, what couldn't he do?" She laughed. "He spied in the lowlands, took messages to Spain, he even played the monk. I was only a pip *then*. But such a life! When he was just a stripling he went a-soldiering for a mighty lord. Oh, was that a terrible man! His only lordly thought was to get back his magical Tooth—"

"A Dragontooth?"

"Oh yes, can you imagine? He told Johnny it rightwise belonged to his domain. My Johnny made up a plan for him—There's some good Spanish port if you like, or shall I go on?"

"Go on."

"Such a plan! And it worked, all right, and they got it. He wrapped it and bound it and had Johnny take it back safe to his lordly lands. 'Course Johnny went off to Turkeyland next (I don't know why), and forgot the Tooth. And then Spain, as I've said, and all over. It took him years, but he finally made himself a name, and the king sent for him, and he charged Johnny to find him the four treasures. What were they? Let's see: the philosopher's stone; the unicorn's horn; the. . . ." She gestured at the stone.

"Periadam?"

"Yes, well, what you have in your hand—and the self-same Dragontooth. Well, Johnny took the job because he knew right off where to go for the Tooth."

"And where was it?"

"Me, know? Seven times never! That lord was a rakehell and everything about the Tooth was mum. But let me finish. Johnny was as smart as a thief, but he couldn't never find a way to slip it away. So what could he show for his troubles? Well, a picture is better than nought, said he, and he made himself a picture of the tooth and had it printed to give to the king. Of course you know our black-hearted lord found out, and what do you think he did? He sent men to hunt Johnny down and cut off his hand!"

"Cut off his hand?"

"Aye, for drawing his tooth. And they went to the printshop and smashed up the block and the pictures that they found. Johnny came back without tooth, or picture, or hand. Poor Johnny."

"And what was the year of this terrible tale?"

"Oh, I wouldn't know. Before I met Johnny." Then a look of bewilderment clouded her plain features. "Why did they kill him now? We lived a good life on this hill."

"But who killed him?"

"Who? I don't know. *'Into the closet!'* cried Johnny when they came to the door. They wanted that Tooth. But he wouldn't tell them nought, so they took his poor life." She heaved a sigh. "Does it all balance in the end? The sweetness and the sorrow?"

"It does," said Ibn, who had said not a word.

"Then enough of my sorrows," she said. "You haven't come from some far away palace just to comfort weeping widows, have you? What did you want from old John?"

"Lady, we too seek the Dragontooth. And if we can, to right a wrong."

"Lord," said she, "such kind souls to dance into a lion's den. Would that I could tell you more." Then her face brightened. "And I shall. Do you know who knows more than anyone of such affairs? The Druids. And if you cannot find a Druid, the Bards will do."

"Then who is the greatest bard, and where shall we find him?" I asked.

"There are many, and who could judge among them? Colm? Flain? Ruman Wydd? But go to the Court, they'll all be there."

"The Court?"

"The Court of the Bards, what a gathering it is, and there's one held this very year. Go, you'll not regret it." She frowned. "But I do not know where it is now held. But any wise, if this is your path, you'll learn it."

"That I too believe," said I. "Now listen. Today you have done more good than you know, but henceforth guard your tongue!" She nodded. "Ibn," I said, "we must leave now if we would make the gates before dark. Good woman, let me give you something for your pains." And I laid five coins on her mantle so that she could not see that they were gold. Halfway down the hill Ibn turned to me. "My lord, what power you have to loosen tongues! If it is a gift, I hope it comes from God!"

October the 12th

What a gathering! Travelers and gypsies, wild black Celts, rogue pilgrims, tinkers, traders, stargazers, and fools all spread out across a great meadow like the Macedonian legions. We made camp where the field bordered a forest, watered our mules, and let ourselves wander. There were a score of nomad tribes, each with their wagons and tents drawn up to form their own quar-

Station XIV
The Court of the Bards

ter. Pavilions and booths had been raised, and the rich. odor of sizzling garlic filled the air. Jugglers strolled about, wantons plied their trade from curtained bowers, and from around every corner came the strain of harp and rattle and hand drum. Taking in the excitement, Ibn turned to me. "Truly, my lord," he said, "only destiny can guide us now."

At one end of the field a stage had been erected with banners and twining laurel leaves. There were bardic contests and much ado, speeches, songs and ceremonies, but yet no sign that spoke of dragons.

The Court ends tomorrow. Circumambulating the meadow, looking for I knew not what, I passed a knot of gypsy women watching an Irish sword dance. One of them broke away and took me by the wrist. It was Doona, who had prophesied by the stream! "Come, my lord," she said. "Now I shall take you to Y Derwydd," and she led me through the press and toward a thicket where two burly men with staffs lounged in the sunlight. Doona nodded at them and took a track that headed into the forest. They paid us no mind. Hawthorn and berry-brambles gave way to giant forest beech. Finally, I made out a clearing up ahead. My guide stopped.

"Touch ground when Y Derwydd greets you. Stand or sit as he says. Ask a question only if you will take the answer. Do not anger Y Derwydd, for the wrath of Derwydd follows a man through many lives. Do not turn your back to Derwydd, it is insolence. Touch ground again when you leave, and be thankful that the gods have brought you here."

"Woman," I said, "what does Y Derwydd mean? Is it a name, or a title?"

She looked at me as if I were a child or a fool. "*The Druid.* He is the oldest and the last; he is called Dagd Dé." Then she led me into the clearing and sat me upon a rough hewn bench. The space was bathed in warm sunlight and filled with birdsong. In the center was a large thatched hall, newly erected. Men in coarse-wove robes went about their business. At mid-afternoon I was summoned to Y Derwydd. I was not disappointed. He sat tall and solemnly white-robed upon a carven throne of oak at the rear of the room. In one hand he held a staff set with a polished black stone. The old man's eyes fell upon me, but he made no sound. A tranquil darkness emanated from beneath his shaggy brows. My questions all sunk into oblivion under the weight of his gaze. In their stead I felt an urge to abandon the pursuits of life, to give myself to silence, to a warm and endless dark.

Yet I knew this longing as false. There was a camphored smell of death about it. With a force of will, I bowed, breaking the gaze and touched the ground. Y Derwydd nodded gravely.

"You are not one of us, New-man. Neither the fire nor the knowledge is in you. The old high honors do not sing in your blood." He stroked his staff. "Yet our fates are linked." He pointed a long finger at me. "Though you are no longer young, you are still vital and you have turned your will to wisdom. The time once was when we would feast and honor you as one sent by the gods, crown you with mistletoe, and then open you that your blood would flow ruby upon the altar and your spirit find a home in some mossy oak. But those days are gone, and shall return no more."

"My lord," I said, "I am merely a pilgrim on a holy search. In the end all trails have led to you, chieftest and wisest of your order, whose counsel alone may illuminate the darkness before me."

"Go, New-man," he rumbled. "I am not your lord, nor are we an *order*. We are the Ancient Ones! Before the ships of the Tuatha Dé Danaan foundered on the emerald shores, we had awoke. When the Fomorians hunted these dappled valleys with gold-tipped spears, we rejoiced. When the Kings arose in painted halls, we whispered the future in their ears and were honored. But in these lesser days we only mourn. How can we have business, you and I?"

"Even then, will not the wise counsel if it is to their advantage? Hear me out, Y Derwydd."

"You seek instruction, do you not? In the matter of a Quest?" I stared at him, for I had told no one there of my purpose. "You have taken quest for the Perilous Tooth, have you not! How could I not know?" He smiled for the first time, a forbidding smile. "Do not think I am some wan Christian priest seeking alms and advantages. Now go."

I took a step backwards and stood not knowing what to do. Then, as happened before, my hand lifted of its own accord to the secret jewel that hung around my neck. Touching it, a fire flowed into my spirit. I cast off my wrap, and, lifting the Periadam before me like a badge of authority, I addressed him with a ringing voice I did not know I possessed.

"O Dagd Dé: Know that this is no day of bartering. I am not a merchant in the market, but the holder of the Periadam that does not diminish. Behold the Secret Stone! It strips you of all lesser bonds and

116

oaths, Dagd Dé. I stand before you as ambassador of the Master Eugnostos, whose wisdom spans the seven heavens and the seven hells, and he has spoken."

The words echoed around the room. Y Derwydd gripped his staff, and motioned with it toward a large rounded stone that sat opposite his throne. "So be it. Take the Seat of Listening." He slowly raised himself in his throne.

"You seek the Unbelonger, Y Draig Coch, The Red Dragon. How much mischief might have been avoided if the Chú had not dragged those teeth to our green-grown earth. Yet they have come and now the Red Dragon calls to you." He paused. "Very well. You are chosen.

"Now hear what I know of this thing," he said in a greater voice, as if addressing a company of men. "Know, O Magnalucius, that we the Druidecht have always guided the fate of these hallowed isles, even since the Golden Age when years were not counted like pennies in a purse as they are today.

"Out from the Deeps the mighty Chú brought Redtooth back to earth, and passed it to his son Oloi. Generations followed like falling leaves, the Tooth moved from hand to hand until it became our secret treasure: honored, but unused. Then a great tumult rose from the land of Hy, tribe murdering tribe, and Sencha MacAilella arose seeking order for his realm. Cathbhadh was his chief Druid, and the slaughter weighed on him as well. He knew of the Tooth—called also Mangfang the Red—and he secretly came and conferred with his Druid brethren here, that he might borrow the thing. Seeing that he was the wisest of the age, we yielded, and he brought the Tooth to his strife-torn home. There he wielded it for his king, and Sencha pacified the wild warriors, and took the high kingship. Yet in the end their works were undone by Briciu, who was called also the Poisontongue. He was a spell-weaver, and burned for the Y Draig Coch. So he found the ear of Sencha and then Cathbhadh, and neither could perceive the workings of his gossip, and he turned them against each other and a veil of confusion fell over the court. Thus Briciu was able to gain the Perilous Dragontooth for which you search.

"In the end Briciu was unmasked and pursued by the Great Assembly, the Mordhhail Uisnigh of the Druidum, and fled northward where he sought refuge on a barren isle. But knowing there was no hiding from Cathbhadh and his hundred men, he concealed the Tooth

Agon magnum erat in Kokanius nanus erat magister caeli, et spiritum Drommi extraxit ad confligendum super agros praelii. Ubique contre maerant homines cum timore de ignis alalantibus.

— Sed fortitudo Drommi erat sub terra in stirpe, in saxo, in rivalo. Pedam post pedem duxit magnum nanogum in locum sacrum. Ibi super cortinam certabant faciem, donec in finem erat druidis fortior in voluntate et super alteram praedabatur.

Verba haec ultima relatas est sicut narrationem eius finitas, et sedebat tacitum in aula tenebrosa.

— Finisne est Dand de — dixit inquirens — Alia narranda sunt, sed facile finitavo non mihi omnia relevanda tibi.

Quis alias mihi hoc narrare potest — druidis.

— Fides in silentium occiderant — inquit — sed mihi instatis sine cessatione. Audi me, Neander. Post alia latus et post victoriam V. Drag Coch, nanus in furias compulsus est et gentem eius in cortinam iactavit. Furiavit et saltavit in furias vestimenta eius duens.

in a secret cave, and bound himself to it with a mighty oath. Then he disappeared from this world."

"Disappeared?"

"Yes. The Druidum pledged to hunt him down wherever he walked on earth, so Briciu escaped into the Magh Dá Cheo. It became his home."

"Then did Cathbhadh find the Tooth?"

"No. The Tooth lay quiet; they could not get its scent. The seasons came and went, the years went by. In time it was forgotten.

"But when the Saxon fell upon this island the Druid host were near undone by a secret strength we could not match. Then we learned that in their far-off native land, a sorcerer-dwarf had found Whitefang, the second Tooth of Bréwulf. Koranian was his name, waist-high to a warrior, but mighty in cunning and cruelty. He wielded the Tooth as a tool of hate, and he was in the van of the longboats that hammered at our shore. It was by this Tooth, the White Dragon, that the British warrior was undone. It was in that day that Merlinus awoke and called up his king."

"Arthur?" I must have cried aloud. So we had come to the blazing hub of the matter. Even I, from far-off lands, had heard of Arthur.

"The king and his enchanter lifted the spirits of the people. But only when we found Y Draig Coch again did British fortunes change. It was Dromm of the line of Chú who took it from its cave, and brought it back to our shores, and loosed the power of the Red Dragon once more across the land.

"On the field heroes clashed and heroes died, dragons on their standards. But the real battle for this soil was between the Dragon-teeth, red against the white." The Druid's eyes gleamed. "That was a mighty contest! Koranian the Dwarf was a Skymaster, and he drew Dromm's spirit up to clash with him over the battlefields, and everywhere men quaked with fear from the shrieking sounds.

"But Dromm's strength was in the earth, root, rock, and runnel. Step by step he drew the dwarfish necromancer down to his holy grove. There, over a cauldron they strove, face to face—until at last the Druid proved stronger in will and broke the other's mind."

119

These last words he delivered as if concluding the tale, and sat silently in the gloomy hall.

"Is that the end, Dagd Dé?" I asked.

"There is more to the story. But by Finian's eye, it is not my duty to reveal all things to you!"

"Who else can tell the tale, Druid?" said I.

"The harps are still," said he, "but you beat upon my brain. Listen, New-man. When the shrieking stilled, and Y Draig Coch had won, the dwarf became a deranged thing and cast his Tooth into the pot, and raved and danced in fury, tearing off his garments. This was an evil thing to behold, for Koranian the Dwarf was thus revealed as a loathsome hag, and she danced a wild gig, disgustingly exposing herself to him. Her eyes were red and she was obscene and ruined.

"Then Dromm laid a doom upon her that if ever she touched a Dragontooth it would scorch her to the bone. He struck her like a dog, and she ran howling naked among the trees.

"With a last incantation he then laid his Redtooth upon the White, and, wrapping the cauldron with his cloak, he sealed it in a stony tomb, for he was spent and sick of dragon things."

A chill prickled my neck. Was my Quest coming to its end?

"No," he said, as if he heard my thoughts, "the matter does not end. The Saxon was beaten, and an interlude of peace came to this land, and forgetfulness as well. Dromm passed out of the history, some say to the Western Isles. Koranian the Dwarf lurked on in the grove as a wild animal, and came to be known as Shee, the guardian of the place. The Bards sang only of the deeds of Arthur, and knowledge of the cauldron grew dim, and was lost. Still, when the Northmen returned to gnaw at the land, they could not prevail, for it was as if the Saxon spirit was subject to the British, just as the one tooth lay under the other in Dromm's buried cauldron. But Y Draig Coch is not given to lying still forever. Can you not guess who came creeping back from the fastness of his Misty Plain to claim his Tooth? Deathless Briciu. He found the grove and found the tomb and found the Tooth. Koranian fell upon him and bit off his ear, but Briciu bested her, and took his prize back to his secret cave. And he had not been idle in his exile; he had learnt how to direct the will of the stone-spirits. So commanding them to seal the opening with a great boulder, Briciu returned to his Otherworld."

"Thus the Tooth found its way to the cave. But now the Tooth is gone." I said.

"Ah," said the Druid, with a cold smile, "so you know something of this tale. Where then did it go, New-man?"

"I am here to learn."

"Then listen. In time, the curious of those parts rolled the stone away from Briciu's cave. But shadows dwelt within and spread fear among the people all around. Being foolish, they sought help from your Christian intruders that crawled about the land. Alas for Briciu they found the monk we call Matha's Bane. He came and fasted for forty days, and perceived the Tooth lying secretly in a crack. But when he laid his hand upon it, Briciu did tremble in his Realm, and quickly came to contest the thing. The two strove till finally the monk cast Briciu back to his Plain of Mists. Then he called the powers of Aibellan to seal him there with watch and ward and cross. That monk would have made a mighty Druid! The Tooth he took; the dew-stone he left behind.

"There my story ends. The stone hangs around your neck; the Tooth has wandered out of knowing. But this I will tell you—by force of Dromm's deed, his seat is the thing's true home."

"Then it is there today?"

"Fool of a wanderer, that place is only its *home*. It is like you, it strays and returns according to its fate."

"Then do you see where the Perilous Dragontooth strays today?"

"New-man, do you know why our horns are silent and our altars dry? This is the bitter work of Dragontooth. It casts a hard new light, and our ancient mysteries are naked and undone. Our old vision dims. Perhaps Y Draig Coch has returned to its seat, perhaps not. Now my tongue dries up, New-man, for I have told you hidden and foresworn accounts, you who are not one of us."

"Dagd Dé," said I, "why have you not gone to claim the thing?"

"Fool!" he said. "It has not been idly named the Perilous. When we lost the Tooth, we lost the Toothtamer which now swings around your neck. Will you give it to me now? I think not. Without it we would only become ensnared in its stratagems."

"Then I shall go there and tame the thing. Where is its place?"

He looked at me with disdain. "And you will do this deed? My sight dims, but I am not blind. I think not. No, I have said too much. I will tell you no more."

"Dagd Dé!" I said. "How can I go forth? *In amore Unicornis*, inform me where it lies and be done."

He groaned, and made an effort to speak, but, shaking, spat a gobbit of blood upon the earthen floor instead. "No!" he cried. "Get from my hovel, for I am now an oath-breaker, and dangerous," and he threw down his staff.

At the clatter, his attendants entered. I bowed, touched the ground, and left.

I was shown to the path by which I had come. Doona was there, waiting to escort me back to the field, and to Ibn.

October the 16th

The Court is over, the harps are stilled; the last wagon rolled away, while only our solitary tent remained on the field. Ibn sat mending a bridle, implacable as ever, but I sipped the bitter draught of failure. I have lore enough to write another *Edda*, but no Tooth, no plan, not even a direction. The leaves are turning; winter is not far off. Have we been seeking a shadow? An *elemental virtue*? Overhead a plover wheeled and dove in the last light of the setting sun.

I wandered across to the head of the field to where the six Year-Stones had been ceremonially arranged, and sat upon one. *For now, farewell, through forest and fern; Like Urien's raven, in Six return!* had been the pledge at all the leave-takings yesterday. Perhaps I should have made it too. Then I would be back again, like the Wandering Jew, a wraith eternally circling this land in search of the lost Dragontooth. Back at our camp, a flicker showed Ibn was kindling his evening fire. There was a haunch of mutton left that he would slice, and no doubt he would contrive something warm to drink. He would spread two sheepskin hides for seats and set our bowls upon some shred of clean linen. There, in that little growing circle of light, a higher order proceeded, untroubled by Druids and dragonteeth. I returned, hung my packet-sack of journals on a crooked branch before the tent, and sat by the fire.

Then we heard the thud of horses coming toward us at a hard trot. Ibn pulled his dagger from the meat and slid it into his belt. "Five or six," I said. He nodded. I thought: we are two. If these are hostile men we will be overmatched. The woods are ten paces away. Should we not slip into the forest? Yet I did not move. Instead, I threw an armful of faggots on the fire, and waited. Thus there we sat when five riders heeled up in our ring of light, their horses snorting and tossing on their bits. They were armed—and at their lead was Faust.

He sat easily on a strong speckled gray, and he was no longer dressed in velvet, but in an oiled leather jerkin, and knee-high boots. A saber hung at his side. He shot a glance at my bag, which hung almost within his reach, and gave a grave smile. He was no student of art now.

"So, good pilgrims, indeed we meet again."

I saw Ibn's hand slowly wrap around the handle of his dagger and with my eyes said *no*. We had been outmaneuvered. I would not see his blood shed for nought.

Faust pricked his animal, and sidled it to stand nervously between the bag and me. "We have much to talk about, Magnalucius. Surely you will welcome us to share your fire?"

"Welcome or nay, you already share my fire."

"Were it mine I would surely welcome you."

"No doubt you would. But I tend a different fire than most other men." I spoke deliberately, as if I commanded a great unseen power. It was our only hope.

"Thus the gnostic pilgrim reveals he is a master of the mystic flame? I think not, old friend. But let us not dance around in words, for we are bound together in a fearful intimacy, are we not?

"Perhaps we are bound together, Faust, but not in intimacy. I choose my friends carefully, and I have not yet found a murderer among their ranks."

"Nor I," he grinned coolly. "You misjudge me, Magnalucius. There is much at stake in our game. Sometimes we do what we must."

"And for what we do we will not escape judgment, Faust, neither you nor I, nor the hirelings behind you."

His men remained stone-faced. One of them sucked at his teeth and shifted in his saddle. The jagged cry of a hoot-owl floated across the meadow.

"True enough. But let us not waste words! We have serious business. He gave a nod to his men and they reined their horses a short distance away.

"Magnalucius. You seek a Dragontooth. I seek the same."

I thought of the trail of blood this man had left in his search, but I needed to play for time. "I know not where any Dragontooth is hid," I said.

"I would still hear all that you have learned. Have you spoken to Nemthenga?"

"Nemthenga?"

"You know the Tooth, but not Nemthenga? Well, there is no reason to keep knowledge from you now. Nemthenga is a sorcerer bound to the Tooth."

"Where is he that I might have spoken to him?" I asked.

"He dwells in the Plain of Two Mists. You have been there too—it marks a man."

"But hold! Are we speaking of one also called Briciu?"

"Briciu, Nemthenga, Poisontongue. Yes, those are his names."

"Then how can you ask if I have talked with him? He lived in the times of Arthur and the saints."

"Perhaps you did not understand his tale. Briciu changed places with the Dragontooth. Thus *even now* he abides in the Timeless Realm. He has become part of it, deathless as the Tooth. Are you sure you have not seen him there? He is old and thin and hard. And dangerous."

"Yes," I cried, "I have seen him! Once in a dream he spoke to me, and again I saw him in a vision."

124

"That is his way of reaching us," said the alchemist. "He is locked within that other world. He cannot set foot here again." Faust shook his head sternly. "He crossed one of those mighty saints of old."

"And lost! I know the tale. He was banished from the earth."

"But that is only half the story. After laying that awful curse upon Briciu, Christian remorse overcame the monk. 'I cannot wholly undo what has been done,' he said, 'but by Christ's mercy, this bar shall lift for seven times seven days at the end of each millennium. Begone! Wait for a thousand years to pass since our Savior's birth, then begin your wait again.'"

"Thus," I said slowly, "in the year of our Lord one thousand he must have briefly walked the earth again. But how do you know these things, Faust?" I asked.

He looked at me and a shadow passed over his eyes. "From Briciu."

"Then you have discoursed with him?"

"At length. It was an anguished story. It was a tale from hell."

"Has he repented of his evils? My time with him was short, but he seemed most reasonable."

"Oh yes, that is his skill. But he is a sorcerer—it does not occur to him to seek forgiveness! He rather seeks domain over living souls who freely walk the earth, that through them he may use the Tooth." He paused, as if weighing his words. "And this he proposed to me."

"May God have mercy on your soul!" said I, for now I pitied Faust, even as his men encircled us. "What treasures did he offer that you agreed to such a thing?"

"*Agreed*? You misunderstand!"

"But you search for the Tooth, do you not?"

"Of course. But for my people, not for him."

Ibn stepped up. "No lies, O Faust. Have you not haunted our steps, and sought our lives, and entered our rooms and even murdered in your quest?" I had not seen him in this temper before.

Faust dismounted and faced him. "Yes, I have long pursued your master from afar, for I would know the secrets he has found. But no, by the Triple Flame, I have not sought his or any other's harm."

125

"Then why have you ringed us with steel?" said I.

"You mean these men?" Faust suddenly laughed. "Ah, but now I see your thoughts. No, no, my friends, you are not under siege tonight. But danger stalks your path now, and I am here, with these men at arms to guard you. That is, if you will."

"So that you may seize the Y Draig Coch when it is found? Speak truly now," I cried, "for we serve the Gnostic Brotherhood, and trifling is done."

He tied his horses reins around the crooked sapling on which my sack hung. "Sirs. Let us sit together by your hearth, the better to finish this?" It was not a command, and so Ibn and I joined him by the fire. He found a stick and stirred the coals, so that sparks flew up. "By this fire," he said quietly, then louder, "I call upon this fire as witness, by the earth as witness, by the air and water as witness, and upon the Creator of all: *I seek the Whitetooth*, the Tooth of my people, not the Red. That is my quest. Will you help me? If so, then you shall have my aid to gain the thing you seek!"

"Then it was not your men who attacked us in that darkened street, or waylaid Severinus?"

"Think, man. If that was my plan, I could be done with you right now, and both Teeth would be in my grasp."

"For what purpose do you seek your Tooth, Faust?" I asked.

"It is a tool of knowledge."

"But do you not know, *All knowledge is vain*?" said I.

"*Except where there be work*," he replied.

"*And all work is empty*," said Ibn.

"*Except where there be love*," finished Faust.

So we were bound together after all. Thus Ibn and I made our peace with Faust. We spoke deep into the night and he questioned us closely. Of greatest interest to him was my vision in the dell, and he made me recall to mind the players there. It was Briciu who laid the Tooth within the tomb; that was clear enough. "But who were the men that took both Teeth out?" said he. "Were there flags or shields or any emblem upon their cloaks?"

"I remember the one," said I, "who wore a long gray gown, a white collar at his neck. The other who claimed the Whitetooth had on him a badge that showed three heads in silhouette." At this Faust clapped his thigh in triumph. "Good! Go on!" Thus we went over each station of the Quest, and I marveled, for Faust drew forth from us things that we had forgot, and he interpreted Fondla's illumination, and dazzled us with his knowledge of the histories of this land, and by the first dim light of dawn, we had discerned where to go to find the Y Draig Coch, or Redfang, the Perilous Dragontooth . . . or so I pray. In the morning we shall ride together. Onward!

Station XV
The Perilous Dragontooth

October the 25th

Ibn has found us lodgings hard on Fish Street. Faust and his men are quartered out past the Black-friar's. The Tooth is near. Now we make final calculations. Faust, Ibn, and I pore over my journals. A theory takes shape.

October the 27th

FOUND. Twenty feet, and square, paced and measured, there it was! We have established the Place of the Perilous Tooth! All along we have been guided. By Sophia's brow, the *grand pattern holds to the end. And guarded by Koranian the dwarf!* Ibn and I clandestinely surveyed everything and returned home. We must devise a strategy to seize the Dragontooth. I wait, the time will come.

October the 29th

Today, all day, *the dragon has been watching.* A dozen times I have glimpsed his scaly head emerging from the splotches on an upraised rock or a whorl of bark or pattern on a rug. I look again, and he is gone. Has this world grown thin, revealing the nemesis lurking behind it, spying on me from the Otherworld? Is this a form of madness? *No.* Faust has just warned me that we draw close to Samhain night. I had not heard of it. It is the Night of Old Magic, he says. Not whispers over colored candles, but a river of ancient power that rises over its

banks and spreads between the worlds. It is wise to keep this night in prayer, he says. Is this why I wait? I must gather my meditations.

 Faust came after dinner. He is a wiser soul than I had thought, and is content to wait. "In this matter," he said, "I must trust you. The Periadam hangs around your neck alone, a gift of destiny."

At these words a stab of remorse bit at me. "But I must confess to you it was not a gift!" I said, and recounted how I had purloined it from the Antiquarium. Faust listened carefully.

"Things are not always what they seem," he said. "Your thinking goes awry. A Periadam truly stolen would fail its holder, but yours has been a faithful guide. How else could we have gotten here?"

"But Faust, my path has been a trail of errors."

"My lord," said Ibn, "perhaps the Periadam sees the one you truly are more clearly than you do yourself."

There are moments when the simplest remark is revelation. So it was. Right then I knew my burden was not the search, it was *myself!* My Quest was not so much to grasp the tooth but to loosen my grip on whom I thought I was. I was like a diver who has gathered a great sack of pearls, but, clinging to his hoard, cannot rise to the surface. "I would be alone now," I said, and left our rooms. My feet found the solitude of a nearby commons, and there I stood and lifted my gaze to the stars. A crescent moon had risen over the rooftops, shining like a beacon. The night of Samhain! Perhaps, I thought, there was music echoing among the spheres tonight. Would that I had the ears to hear it! Moon and stars and endless space—they were real, not Magnalucius and his Quest. Let me be the diver who rises up into the air. *Let me be an arrow loosed from the bow*, I thought, *a word, a song, a breath of power*. Without intention I turned and set out across the field.

Samhain. This night was different; it flickered like a torch. I passed a row of elm along the swale, their branches shifting in the night breeze. Dragon shapes struggled to disengage themselves from the leafy shadows, then dissolved into moonlight.

Samhain. The city moved. A different kind of light shone—the preternatural light of the Plain. Was I moving between buildings of rough stone, or rough stone that seemed like buildings? I was moving through *both* worlds, but I was of neither. I was the Watcher again, and I made for the Place of the Tooth.

There were other nightwalkers. I saw a light, and it drew near. It was a cloaked man with a lantern held aloft. He was dressed in red and a golden circlet was upon his brow. His hair was long and lustrous; his face was solemn. It was Master Abaris.

"Magnalucius!" he cried, "How marvelous we meet again, good brother, we who share this Quest. Samhain Blessings to you. Where are you bound on so bold a night?"

"O Abaris," I said, "I come from the Deeps, bound by a holy will." And I saw that he was wholly in the Timeless Plain and could not discern where in the four-square world I trod.

"Well said," spoke he, "And now by fate decreed we are pilgrims meeting on the path. How good it is to walk awhile together on such a reckless night."

"You honor me," I said. "But in this hour I would be alone."

"Who would then intrude into another's purposes, O Magnalucius?" he said. "There are consecrated things that must be done alone. But listen! I am your friend. We are companions now in a secret undertaking. One age is ending, another begins. In this there are works best borne by two, for in companionship is strength. Forces that might break one, two will bear with ease. What do you think?"

"Say on," said I.

"Magnalucius," he continued, his face aglow, "let us seize the day! We enter the age of the Dragon! Too long man has stood befuddled by the workings of the world. A new science can open all God's secrets now—a science proposed long ago, but awaiting the power of the sacred Tooth to flower. You know the work of Bacon? Copernicus? Leonardo? Doctors of this science, all.

"Gaining it man shall gain the vigor of youth, even the pre-
sumptuousness of youth, reducing and dividing all phenomena until
grasping each piece and part, he will encompass the mysterious whole
and see with the eye of God! What might we not accomplish then,
Magnalucius? Hunger and disease? Gone! Old age? Banished! Death?
Yes, Magnalucius, even death will surrender its mysteries. Is not this a
new and holy alchemy? Is this not the work God ordains? Shall we not
take our true home among the stars, and hear the music there?"

As he spoke a bright new world opened to my mind, and I understood in a flash the process by which the mind of man could conquer
nature. Never had I imagined such a fascinating outcome to the trials
of man. His words were music; there was perfume in the air.

Then something moved in the shadows behind Abaris. Shielding
my eyes from the glare of his lamp, I saw couched in the rocks a dark
figure, watching us. "Step forward, friend," I commanded.

To my amazement, Ibn leaped lightly down.

"Ibn! How come you here so quietly, and why?" I asked.

"By Sufa's ways, my lord. For now I have a little part to play."

Abaris's eyes narrowed for an instant. "Who is this Moor? Is he a slave?"

"Slave? Perhaps. But tonight a slave no longer," I said, "for in this night of freedom,
Ibn, I release whatever hold I have on you, and you are free."

"So shall it be," said Ibn. "Tonight that freedom I shall need."
Then he stepped boldly forward so that he stood between us.

Abaris spoke softly. "Magnalucius, a word with—"

"My lord, beware this man," interrupted the Moor, his voice
sounding hard and plain.

"Ibn," said I, "you ill-speak a man with a wide and hopeful vision."

"Yes, my lord," said Ibn, "and a smooth and subtle tongue as
well. But beware his dark and hungry heart!"

"Have care, dear Moor," said Abaris, "for in this land false speech
draws a quick and just reward." Then his tone grew gentle. "But here
likewise blessings come swiftly to the righteous, and I see that you are
that. How feel you Ibn, now your chains are gone? Is not the taste of

freedom sweet? Do not deny the same for all men now. The old order is gone, and new forces seek to ally themselves with men. Will you not aid us? Come, together let us walk down the templed ages."

Ibn grinned, showing his teeth. "Your words are sweet as scented wine, master Abaris. But poisonous, I do fear. Alas, I am only a Blackamoor who has not the wit to know of orders old or new. *But I know the taste of Truth.*"

Then he flung aside his cloak; in his hand was Milesian's shining sword. "There is one other thing I know, O deceiver: that you will not detain my lord with yet another honeyed word. *Not one.* Your life hangs on a thread of silence. Heed me; this is the oath of Ibn Sufa al-Iskandar, and not an idle jest." Then he turned to me. "Go quickly, my lord, the night runs late."

I would heed my friend, for Ibn had broken the enchantment Abaris's words held over me, yet I could not move—I was bound to see the outcome. Seeing my hesitation, the alchemist bowed low to Ibn, then rising, held his eye.

"O noble Moor," Abaris said at last, in the most grave and conciliatory tone I have ever heard, "I yield to you—" but no more, for at these words, with a motion too swift for my eyes to follow, Ibn swung his sword and struck off Abaris's head.

From some great distance a thin and awful wail rose and fell in the night. I stepped back from the dreadful scene before me. The lantern lay on its side, smoking and spilling oil. Ibn knelt and righted the lamp and wiped his blade on the hem of the dead man's cloak.

"His mind was chained to Briciu's will, my lord, and he wished you bound as well. But he should have known I would not break my word." He stood up, and his eyes were fathomless as the night sky. "His judgment today; ours tomorrow! God rewards the righteous, but the blood of three good Christian monks—and nearly ours as well— stained this man's hands. Still, I would that things had not come to such a pass." He slid the blade into its scabbard. "Now go in peace, my lord, but leave the Plain swiftly, there are noisome things abroad tonight." Ibn stood before me for an instant as one of the pillars holding up the vault of heaven.

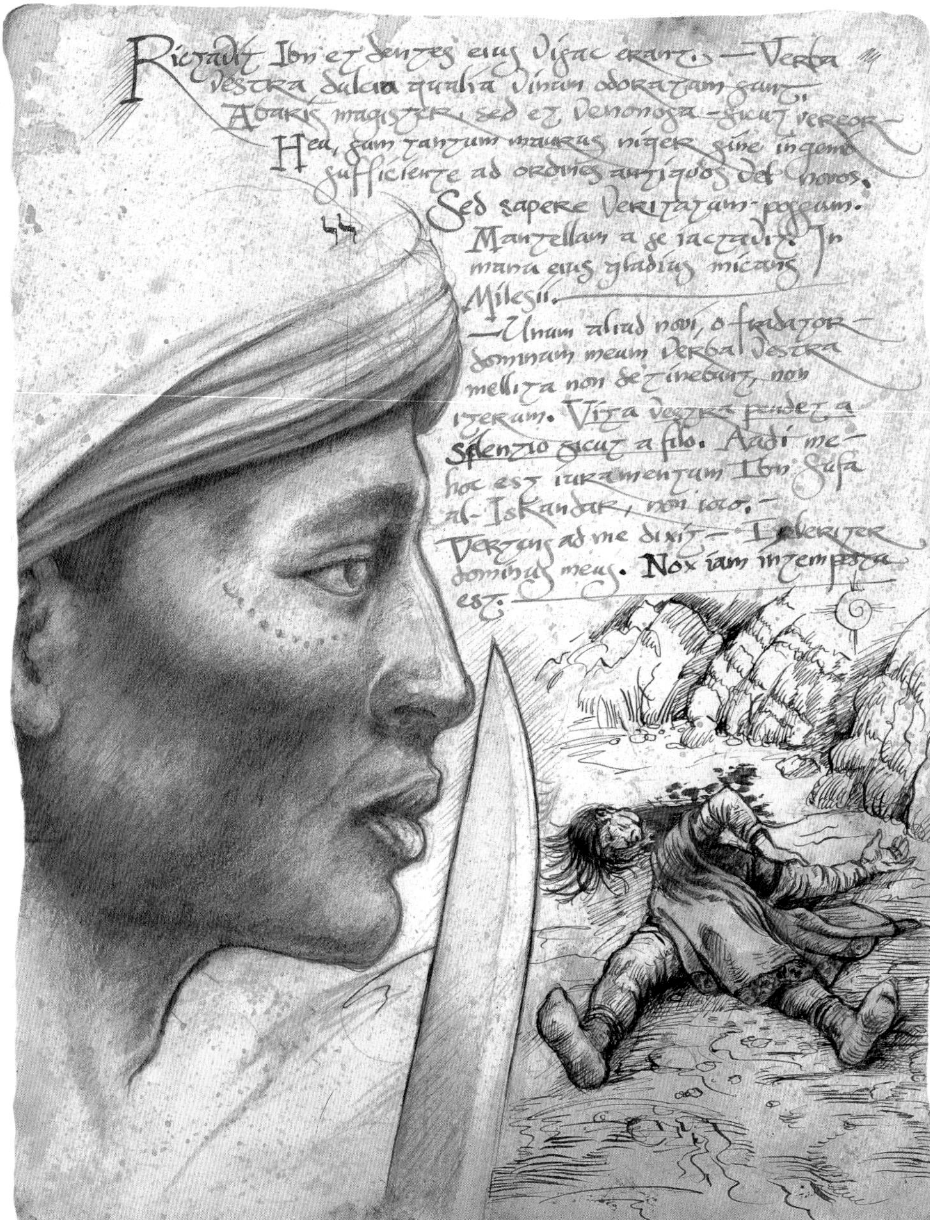

This time I parted quickly. My heart was calm, though I knew not why. Then by the magic of the night I walked out of Brocileande, and proceeded through ordinary cobbled streets to the place of destiny.

It is said *All barriers dissolve before one who walks with God.* Perhaps that is true—I will not make such claim for myself, only that on that night there was no watchman, and all the doors opened easily as I proceeded onward, as in a holy trance. But inside in a darkness illuminated only by thin shafts of Samhain moonlight, I stopped. There before me, moving in the air, alive, I saw the ruby threads! I followed these skeins of fire to their source.

Y Draig Coch. As clearly as if it were before me now I see it in its chest, long and cruel and black in color, like iron—the whitish tip, the pitted root, the handle set with two red stones. Its will beat steadily upon me, but I rode it like a leaf upon the flood. Carefully I grasped the handle and raised the Dragontooth. I could feel a life coursing through it like a rushing stream, and I perceived how the Periadam would capture and transform this force when set at last within the golden clasps.

A clot of dirt lay upon the clasps, and, scarcely thinking, I flicked it away. Lo! in that witless moment the handle slipped from my grasp. Grabbing for it, I seized the naked Tooth itself. A flame coursed up my arm and erupted in my mind. How loud the roar! Chaos embraced me, and I fell into oblivion.

How much later did my senses return? I am not sure. I have fleeting memories of voices, and torches, and hands upon me. After a length of time the creak of a door awoke me, and I sat up. I was in a simple cell, dimly lit. A old man dressed in a long gray gown had entered. He approached the plain bed where I sat and peered at me intently.

"Is it *you?*" he asked.

I looked at him in silence. His broad forehead revealed a life of thought, and though his face was stern the wrinkles around his eyes were not unkind.

He threw open shutters at the far end of the room. There were ornamental bars on the window, but rays of morning light streamed into the chamber. He returned and stood over me.

"What is your name? What do you seek? Why do you seek it?"

The entire adventure had come to a point. "I am called Magnalucius," I said. "I seek Y Draig Coch, the Dragontooth, to unite it with the precious Periadam, and tranquilize the morbid influence which emanates from the thing."

He gave a great sigh. "Then we face each other at last, Magnalucius. I am Fondla the Keeper."

"Fondla, of the Celi Dé?" I cried, and his eyes grew wide for an instant.

"I should have guessed that you would know. Yes, once of the Celi Dé."

"But you are not dead! Then did you. . . ."

"No, I did not steal the Tooth from the Isle. The Tooth was abducted by force. I hid in the sewage drain, then, abandoning my old life, I followed like a hound. I had no choice. You know its powers—it had become a part of me. In time I met its master and gained his trust, and he made me privy to secrets I had not guessed before. Once again I became its Keeper. Now you too have come. But mark, the Dragontooth is no longer a weapon to fragment armies. Magnalucius, think it through completely, as I have. Look around! This is its unquiet age. Invisible, subtle, everywhere, its final work has begun."

"Yes!" I cried, in sudden relief, for I perceived that we were akin in our thoughts. "Your guardianship has been successful, and well met. Release me that together we may effect the holy union and the thing may be tamed and its age concluded."

Yet he only looked at me in silence, and his eyes took on a sadness I could not comprehend. "No," he said at last. "Not yet."

"Not yet?"

"Magnalucius, the Book of Secrets is open now. The *Spiritus Libertatis* of the world has been aroused and *will not rest* until the seven seals are shattered. Do not the signs proliferate daily? Man has exchanged simple faith for the *dragon's mind*. Now he must know everything. And so one day he will. Oh yes, man will harness the powers of thunder and lightning, the raging torrent, the howling wind— new sciences of which we cannot even dream. But how dearly will they be bought, for in their train great engines of destruction will come as well." His voice dropped to a whisper. "And in the end when this

world is flayed and riven for its secrets, man's soul shall wither too."
He shut his eyes. "But of one thing I am most certain: *Within the greatest ill we must still find the Good.* Is this not the divine function? The true alchemy by which lead is rendered into gold? Yes? So now imagine this—imagine that perhaps all this is written in God's holy Plan. *Omni quia sunt, lumina sunt.* All that Is, Is Light!"

"How could this be?" I asked. "Does not the Holy One desire only good for man?"

"Indeed," said he, "but the Divine Mind thinks in great waves of time, not only in the little ripples wherein we bob up and down. By destiny the Perilous Tooth is the tool of a sacred plan by which man shall walk into the Shadow that he may one day *in full knowledge* choose the Light.

"Here is what I propose, Magnalucius. Man's will is now directed to taste forbidden fruit, and he will not cease his gnawing till he bites its bitter core. Yes? Then Christian charity would lead us to make the passage quick, *to leave the Tooth unbound for now and speed its destined work.*"

I looked out the window a long time. Little children played on a lawn outside. "I find no flaw in your argument," I said at last, "but I fear where it will lead. Are you the vehicle for the Tooth?"

"Not I! Nor king, nor pope, Magnalucius. The age of the Prince is done. This power must be broadcast to all." His eyes brightened. "And yes, high beauties and unsought blessings will come out of this as well." He took a deep breath. "Magnalucius, would you show me the Stone?" His hands trembled.

I reached under my cloak and produced the shining Periadam.

"Ah!" he cried. "There it is, sweet dew of the Unicorn. Light of the Firstcomer, the Friend. Lost so long, and now I gaze upon you."

I lifted the orb from around my neck and placed it in his hand. His trembling ceased. He sighed, and tears welled in his eyes.

"I have guarded the Tooth too long," he murmured at last. "Too long I have wrestled with history and peered into the end of days. Now I remember something else. *Something simple.* But how did the blessed Periadam come to you?"

"By the grace of my master Eugnostos."

His eyes grew wide. "What?" he cried, "Eugnostos? Across reign and ruin, I should have known. But is he still alive? How do you know him? How does he fare?"

"He still picks his teeth and spits his olive pits," said I. "Yet by the holy Logos he has attained a perfected state. He is light now, more light than flesh. But how is it that—" In an instant, another tesserae of the pattern was revealed. "But you are Valentinius, the wandering one!"

"I am," said he, "and I have followed a winding path. Magnalucius, do you think he would receive me again?"

"How not so?" said I. "I strayed for sixteen long years, and he received me back as if I had been gone but a day."

He gazed again into the Periadam as if it would measure the truth of my words. Then he kissed the shining globe and handed it to me.

"Here," he said, "freely you gave it to me, freely it returns. And freely do now what thou will to the Perilous Dragontooth."

"I do not understand."

"I have spoken so easily of trusting the immanence of God's holy will. So now I must trust that His Will shall work through you. If I am a servant of destiny, then you are one as well. I resign the Tooth to fate. You have heard the argument, you have weighed it between heart and mind. Do the Joining or not as you will."

It was as if I sat and watched myself at this moment from a lofty tower. Had the hour come to join the Periadam to the Perilous Dragontooth? Or nay?

The sound of the children's laughter drifted to us from outside, and sweetly like an angel's voice came the sing-song words of some childish game: *As in Egypt and Galilee / Let it go and then be free.* Gradually the laughter faded.

The grand pattern held.

I did not move. "His Will be done," I said. "I yield."

In the golden light of morning, motes of dust gently drifted, sparkling like tiny gems.

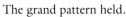

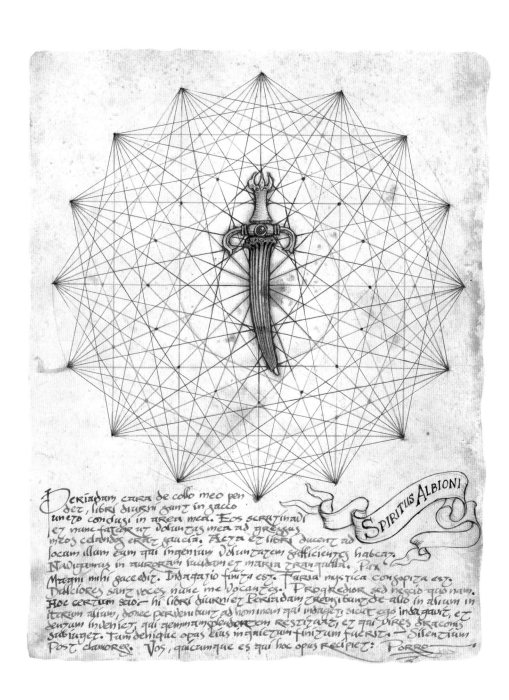

Deriadam cura de collo meo pen
det, libri diurni sunt in sacco
unero condidi in arca mea. Eos scrutinavi
et nunc fateor ut voluntas mea ad gressus
meos celandas erat cautia. Acta et libri ducent ad
locam illam cum qui ingenium voluntatem sufficientes habcat.
Navigamus in auroram suidon et maria tranquilla. Pax
Magni mihi succedit. Indagatio finita est. Faria mystica conspiza est.
Dulciores sunt voces nunc me vocantes. Progredior sed nescio quo nam.
Hoc certum scio—hi libri diurni et Deriadam transibunt de alio in alium in
iterum alium, donec pervenibunt ad hominem qui indager sicut ego indagavi, et
ventum inveniet, qui gemma splendorem restituat, et qui vires draconis
subiuget. Tum denique opus eius in galetum finitum fuerit.— Silentium
Post clamorem. Vos, quicumque es qui hoc opus recipiet: Porro

SPIRITUS ALBIONI

On a Venetian Coasting Vessel Bound for Rome with a Cargo of Wool

Sixteen days ago, we bade goodbye to Johann Faust and boarded Anselmo's ship. Last night, we passed the Pillars and entered the Middle Sea. I rose in the sacred hour before dawn, as is my custom, and seated upon the ship's prow, I watched a family of dolphins pace us in the failing moonlight. Ibn had spread his prayer-mat upon the deck. Far behind us, a new Keeper guarded the Perilous Dragontooth. In a tiny cabin below me, Brother Fondla, once Valentinius, slept like a babe and dreamt, perhaps, of unicorns. The rim of the eastern sky was a-glow, but above, the night sky still ruled, hung with a silver crescent moon in whose pocket lay the glittering morning star. In an earthier darkness another lune held the Y Draig Coch now. Was it a mistake to move it? No. We had shifted it only a few paces, but it was now far safer than where I had so easily laid my hands upon it—and its new place spoke of the great pattern: *Cooled and tempered by good English soil, warmed by the sun on the southern Quadrature; beneath the midpoint of the inner aspect of the lune; outside the square. . . .* Surely a place most suitable for the work before it, a dragonish place indeed.

The precious Periadam hangs about my neck, the journals lie bound in an oiled bag within my trunk. I have examined them carefully and see that my efforts to conceal my tracks were halfhearted. The record will guide one of sufficient wit and determination to the Place. We sail into a clear dawn and calm seas. A great peace has settled over me. The Quest is over, the mystic fever healed. There are sweeter callings now. I am moving onward. I know not where.

Of this I am sure: these journals and the Periadam will pass to another, and another and another, until they come to one who, taking up the Quest, shall find the Tooth, restore the Shining Stone, and quench the Dragonpower. Then shall its unquiet work be done.

Silentium post clamores.

To you, who are that one, Onward!

Unicornis Hortus

Cornu saxum sterilem ferit, profunde perforans, ex illo torrentes
aquas evocans. Quocumque illae aquae pervenirent, extinctae sunt
ignes. Sata est terra florentium multitudine. Arbores magnae
crescebant et florescentes, sub quorum umbris habitabant bestiae, et
ferae et aviles. Haec omnia facta sunt secundum voluntatem Magici.
Unicornis vero instrumentum voluntati eius erat. Perfectus est

igitur Unicornis hortus, qui vocatur Shamayim, id est locus in
quo aquae

Hagios deinde primogenitam locatus est dicens: SOLA INTER CREATURAS
ORIGINES VESTRAS REMINISCERIS ET MANEBIS SEMPER MEMOR
HUIUS LUMINIS, SED NUMQUAM AD LUMEN REVERTES ITAQUE AD HORAM
ULTIMAM HUIUS SAECULI

Et habitabat Ayalam in hortu suo et foris ambulabat magna
cum miratione

Little is now known about author and illustrator **Michael Green** other than that he has been, at times, a sign painter, landscaper, television art director, and drum maker. He lives and works and attempts to unravel life's mysteries in a farmhouse somewhere in Pennsylvania's Brandywine Valley, together with his wife Sally, son Kabir, and truck Toyota.